MEETING HIM·IN·THE WILDERNESS

A TRUE STORY OF ADVENTURE AND FAITH

MEETING HIM·IN·THE WILDERNESS

LOIS ELLEN OLSON

I will court her again, and bring her into the
wilderness, and speak to her tenderly there.
There I will give back her vineyards to her,
and transform her Valley of Troubles into a
Door of Hope. She will respond to me there,
singing with joy as in days long ago in her
youth. . . . (Hosea 2:14-15)
THE LIVING BIBLE

Abingdon / Nashville

MEETING HIM IN THE WILDERNESS

A Festival Book

Copyright © 1980 by Lois Ellen Olson

Festival edition published February 1982

Published by arrangement with Doubleday & Company, Inc.

ISBN 0-687-24261-4

*This book is dedicated to
the Glory of God
in gratitude for
His love and care*

FOREWORD

Lois Olson has a great story to tell. It is a story of high adventure, powerful drama, unforgettable beauty, and profound spiritual depth.

It is the true story of a successful couple with two beautiful children who decide to sell their home, leave the security of the familiar, and move to a tiny, remote community in the Pacific Northwest North Cascade Mountains. The community, Stehekin, is at the north end of majestic Lake Chelan. There are no roads in or out. It is accessible only by boat and small seaplanes.

Lois shares this unique, powerful journey. Her skill in painting word pictures allows us to join them in their hilarious journey across the country to the little one-room schoolhouse where her husband taught. We see the great mountains, hear the roar of the rivers, smell the fresh, clear air, taste the berries, pause at the mountain flowers, walk in awe across the glittering snow in full moonlight.

There is an inner journey that is shared. God has a great plan for ministry for Tom and Lois Olson. Slowly, painfully, the points of contact are made that move them beyond a nominal, conventional faith to deep commitment to Jesus Christ and obedience to the call to preaching and pastoral ministry.

There is the inspiring account of answered prayer as their little daughter, Amy, badly hurt by a blow on her head from a bat swung at the wrong moment, seems to be dying in their arms.

This is a book that will make you laugh and cry. It will leave pictures of stunning beauty in your mind. It will point to the possibilities of high adventure and inspiring faith that await us in our own lives. Reading the book is a spiritual experience.

I am glad you are sharing in this unforgettable journey.

Dr. Joe A. Harding, Senior Pastor
Central United Protestant Church
Richland, Washington

The conviction grew until I could no longer ignore it.

"Write this book for me," He said to me.

"What book, Lord?"

"Tell the story of how I took you to Stehekin when you and Tom were not at all committed to Me. Tell how I wooed you to Me. Tell of your struggles and your triumphs while you learned to trust Me. Tell how I called your husband to be a man for Me and a minister to My people. Tell of your wilderness experience that brought you into the Promised Land."

"All that, Lord? But I can't do that. Those were painful times. You want me to share all that pain? You want me to share all the triumphs, too? But, Lord, that's pretty risky. It's not easy to open yourself up and let people look inside of you. What if they laughed at me or rejected what I said? Lord, that would hurt."

"I know. I gave Myself and was rejected. But that's not the end of the story."

"You're right, Lord. I guess it is worth the risk if it could bring just one person to You and Your blessings. So—what do I write?"

I began to pray about what should go into this book. I asked the Lord to bring to my memory the incidents that would tell the story He wanted told. As I recalled these things, I began to get excited. This would be a great testimony for the Lord. Many people would be able to see what the Lord had done for us. Surely they would see that He would do all this and more for them, too. I began to like the idea of writing a book. And then the Adversary struck.

"Here you go again, Lois. You don't learn very quickly, do you? You certainly have great delusions about yourself. My, my. You, the big, famous author. The great emissary for God. Ha! That makes me laugh!"

I shuddered at the sound of the laughter.

"But the Lord asked me to do this for Him," I said quietly.

"Did He really? I think not. I think you just want to have a great ego trip."

"No. That's not true. I've been through that before, and I cannot do this for an ego trip. You are wrong!"

"Well even if God really did tell you to do this, you still couldn't do it. You don't have the discipline to sit down day after day at the typewriter and little bit by little bit tell the story that took four years to live. You don't have the discipline."

"You are right, Evil One. I don't have the discipline. The Lord will have to provide it."

"All right, so He gives you discipline. But you don't have the talent to write a book."

"You are right again. I don't have the talent. The Lord will have to provide it."

"So what! So He gives you discipline and talent. Who says that what you have to say is worthwhile? Just what makes you think you can say anything that will bring blessing to anyone?"

I couldn't answer that question, so I asked the Lord to confirm it to me. "Lord, I need to know from other people that I really do have something to say that will be a blessing to them."

The next day at church I was standing in the narthex. A woman came up to me and said, "Mrs. Olson, I've been wanting to tell you. Last week when you spoke at our Women's Fellowship luncheon, you really blessed my heart. Your story is such a blessing. I hope you can come again and tell more of it."

Before I could respond to her, two more ladies came. "Your talk was just wonderful. You were talking just to me, you know," said one lady.

"No she wasn't. She was talking to me! She said exactly what I needed to hear," said her companion.

And then the clincher. A fourth lady stepped up to me.

"Mrs. Olson, my name is Lorraine. I was at the luncheon when you shared with us. It really meant so much to me. I have a very dear friend whose husband is dying, and she must stay with him at his bedside. I tried to tell her some of what you said, but you know I can't tell it like you did. She said to me, 'Please ask her for me if she has that written down. If it was only written down, I could read it, you see, and then I could be blessed even if I can't get out to hear her speak.'"

Was Lorraine ever surprised when tears welled up in my eyes and I gave her a hug.

"Lorraine, you have just been a blessing to me. You have allowed God to use you to answer my prayer. Thank you. Please tell your friend that my story is not written down yet, but it will be as soon as I can get the words on paper."

And to the Evil One I said, "In the name of Jesus, be gone. You are powerless. This book is the Lord's, and it will be written, not because of who I am, but because of who He is. Hallelujah!"

ACKNOWLEDGMENTS

There are so many beautiful people who have contributed to the writing of this book. First and most important is the Helper Himself, who supplied me with the inspiration, energy, and the very words themselves.

I also want to express my love and appreciation to the people of Stehekin, who allowed us to share their valley and their lives for four years. Thank you for helping us to grow and for putting up with us while we did. May your lives be filled with God's blessings.

There are many of God's special people in Richland, Washington, who helped me write this book. They believed I could do it and prayed continually that I would do it. An especially loving thanks to the Tuesday Group. I also am deeply grateful to Helen Henshaw for beginning the typing for me; Mary Kosky for her great gift in typing the whole first draft and correcting all my horrid spelling errors; Martha Zimmerman for her understanding and encouragement; Lucy Harding for the use of her counseling room to write during the long marathon weekend; Bill McCue, Jr., for the reproduction of the first draft; and especially Joe Harding for his advice, enthusiasm, affirmation, and numerous prayers over the phone when the going was tough; Russell and Julia Bridges for the prayer support and use of the summer house for the writing of the final draft in Atlanta, Georgia; and to Poppie, Tom's dad, for being my "official grammarian."

My deepest gratitude and love goes to my precious family,

Tom, Sally, and Amy, who lived this with me and then still lived with me and loved me while the story was being written.

Tom, marrying you was the most wonderful thing that ever happened to me. Your love and caring for me all these years have enabled me to take long strides on my journey to becoming what God has in mind for me and for us. I love and admire the father that you are; and besides all that, you're a terrific cook! Your typing of the final draft made me feel loved and appreciated. The typing is done now, so the girls can set the table for dinner, and after dinner you can study in peace. I love you.

Lois Ellen Olson

Atlanta, Georgia
January 1979

MEETING HIM·IN·THE WILDERNESS

1

Lightning ripped through the dark early-morning sky. Thunder rumbled and groaned. Rain came in great, blowing drenches. I strained forward over the steering wheel, trying to see the narrow, twisty Ohio country road. The wipers were darting back and forth, slapping at the rain, but I could see only a short distance ahead.

I groaned and spoke to my two-year-old daughter lying on the seat next to me. "Nothing like a midwestern summer storm. But why this morning?"

Amy didn't answer me.

Another flash of lightning revealed the back of a U-Haul truck lumbering along the road ahead of me.

I sighed and relaxed a bit.

"Well at least we aren't lost. Your daddy is ahead of us."

Still Amy didn't answer. In the next flash of lightning I saw that the child on the seat was sleeping. In one hand was the ruffled edge of the ever-present Blankie, and cradled in the other arm was her cloth Baby.

I had to smile at her total lack of concern.

We drove on, creeping slowly around curves. Farm fields stretched out on both sides of the road. The rain and wind slackened, and I could see the U-Haul again, with its gentle sway. "It looks like an elephant laboring along," I thought. And yet for us it was more like a turtle because it was carrying what was left of our home.

As I watched, the truck slowly started off the road. Before I could really wonder what was happening, a neon light flashed brightly in the dark: CAFE, EAT.

I followed the U-Haul into the parking area, glad for a chance to stop, and pulled up next to it. My husband, Tom, jumped down from the driver's seat and started toward me. Sally, our five-year-old, dashed around the side of the truck and ran toward the door of the cafe. A big bump under her jacket and a teddy bear foot sticking out below the jacket showed Smokey was going in also.

"Come on and get a cup of coffee," Tom shouted to me through the window of the pickup I was driving. The flashing EAT sign revealed a wet but grinning face.

He opened the door. "Hurry. It's wet out here."

"Amy's asleep," I said.

"Well wake her up," he shouted as he headed around to the other side of the pickup. I unlocked the door. He reached in and gathered Amy and Blankie and Baby up in one big swoop and ran toward the cafe.

Bright lights, loud, twanging country music, and the smell of bacon and coffee greeted us. We plopped into a booth and ordered coffee, milk, and donuts from the friendly waitress.

"What a way to begin our great adventure," I said to Tom. "We've been driving less than an hour and a half, and we're stopped already."

"We have lots of time. We don't have to be to the boat company till next Wednesday. This is only Thursday," Tom assured me. "We'll just wait here awhile. Maybe this storm will pass soon. At least it will be light shortly, and that will help."

Half an hour later we stepped outside again and found the storm was reduced to a drizzling rain. A faint pink glow shone in the eastern sky as we pulled out onto the road again.

"Well, this is better," I said to Amy. She was on her knees, looking out the back window at the sunrise.

She quickly tired of that and sat down again. "Where are we going, Mommy?" she asked.

"To our new home," I said.

"Oh." She plopped Baby down and started digging through the bag of toys we had brought for her.

The road had straightened out, and the rain had nearly stopped, so I let my mind jump ahead to our new home. We were moving from a big city in Ohio to an isolated mountain village in Washington State. Tom had been a schoolteacher for nine years, the last five in a prestigious private girls' school. We had bought an older home and had had great fun and some pain in fixing it up. We had lovely maple furniture bought in the days before our children were born, when I also taught school. We had friends and fun, lots of activities and service projects. It was a great life. And yet something was missing. Something inside us both kept calling to us, saying, "There is something else. There is more; this is not all there is to life."

There were times in our nine years of marriage that the call was strong. Shortly after our wedding we applied to join the Peace Corps, but my health prevented it. Other times this calling was very quiet, and we even forgot it in all our activity. Then one summer Tom was offered a summer job as a ranger in Yosemite National Park in California. We packed up and went cross-country in five days, no small accomplishment considering we had a three-year-old and a two-month-old and all the paraphernalia associated with young children. Besides that we made the trip in a VW.

We lived that summer in a tenthouse at an elevation of forty-five hundred feet. I cooked on a wood-burning stove. We had one faucet with cold water and a flush outhouse we shared with the other rangers assigned to the Wawona area. For three months we literally lived outside. The evening campfires brought deep sharing and caring among all of us in camp. On Tom's days off we tramped through the woods and wandered along streams. That summer the call inside us grew so loud we could not disregard it. There was something more to life. We were sure of it. But what was it? How did we find out? We didn't know the answer to either question, but one thing was sure: That summer we knew we would have to find the answer.

When we returned to the city in September, we felt ourselves deeply frustrated by everything that we had enjoyed before. We remembered the peace and excitement of our days in the mountains and woods.

"We've got to go back," Tom declared. "There must be a way we can go back and live there for more than just a summer. The answer is back there someplace."

He was educated as a teacher, with both B.S. and master's degrees. He enjoyed teaching, and it was the only way he knew how to earn his living. So he began looking for schools situated in the mountains. He found a book published by the Department of Health, Education, and Welfare that listed every school in each state, the number of students, and the number of teachers. For weeks Tom poured over this book and a map of the western United States. He found the little towns and villages in the mountains from the Canadian border to central California. If the village had a one- or two-room school, he wrote them a letter, including his résumé. One hundred and fifty letters and two years later I put an ad in the newspaper: "Moving to a cabin in the mountains. Nearly everything must be sold. Come to the sale."

For three weekends I stood in my beautiful home and watched as people bought and carried out most of our lovely things. My material heart broke the first day when my gorgeous maple hutches were carried away. At that moment I realized the old life was over. There was only the going forward left.

We saved what we needed and what we knew would fit into the cabin we had seen on our interview trip to the Washington State wilderness area. These things, plus many supplies, were now packed in the U-Haul and the pickup we had bought for the new way of life.

Our new home was located at the end of a glacier-fed lake that wound its way between steep mountains. The lake was fifty-five miles long, and the community we were headed for was at the end of the lake. The mountains were so steep that no roads could be built to this place. The only way to get there was by boat or floatplane. The community had only thirty-five people, no telephones, no TV reception, no grocery, no church. One of its features made us think long and hard before we accepted the job: There were no medical facilities. When one became sick, one had to go to the other end of the lake to the doctor. The only way to get there was by the ferry that traveled the lake. It made a trip once a day in the summer but only three times a week in the winter. The floatplane flew on demand if the weather permitted. What would we do if one of our children got sick or injured? This was an especially big hurdle for me because I had had polio as a child and had required extensive medical services for most of my life. Was it wise for us to deliberately isolate ourselves from immediate help? And yet the people who lived there coped with the situation. The call within us was so loud that we had to take this risk, so I bought a box of first aid supplies, cough medicine, ointments, and the like, and our pediatrician gave me an excellent book.

During the three months we made our preparations to leave the city, Tom and I had become professional list makers. We had been advised to take at least a six-month supply of groceries into the mountains. It never occurred to me even to think how much food we used in six months. And what about toothpaste and toilet paper and razor blades? I began keeping a list of everything we used for a month. I multiplied by six and hoped that would do it. Then we began to buy. We had sold the house and put most of the cash in savings, and the rest we allotted for supplies. We bought case after case of everything. Our house began to look like the storeroom of our local Safeway market. We bought items we had never even dreamed we'd ever use until now, such as snowshoes. Our new house would be heated only by wood, and I would be cooking with wood. Tom would have to cut about eleven cords of wood. A chain saw was at the top of our list.

We took games, craft supplies, sewing supplies, our stereo and records, my guitar. We took lots of candles because we had been told that the electrical power was often erratic during the winter. We had also been informed of the mail-order library service from Wenatchee, so we did not need to take a large number of books.

As people began to see the supplies pile up in our house and saw the VW replaced with a pickup truck, they began to take us seriously.

"You can't really be serious about this move!" one friend gasped. "You must be insane to even think of it."

Other people sorrowfully shook their heads and walked away as though we were walking straight to the guillotine. One neighbor looked at the pictures we had taken on our interview trip and agreed that it was indeed a beautiful place. He smiled kindly and said, "I can understand you might enjoy it, but that sort of thing is not for me."

I wanted to hug him. At least he saw that we might not be like he was and that our needs and his were different but that that didn't make us nuts. That was important to me because there were moments in the middle of the night when I would wake up remembering something to add to our lists. I would wander around the half-empty house stacked with boxes, the moonlight streaming in on the snowshoes and chain saw, and a fit of doubt would grab me. But the morning sun burned away the doubt.

I called my parents in Florida as soon as Tom had received the contract. I very carefully told them where we were going. I got to the part about the thirty-five people, and Mother interrupted.

"Thirty-five what? Hundred thousand?"

I didn't answer.

"Thousand?"

Still no answer.

"Hundred?" Her voice was quiet.

"No, Mother. Just thirty-five. Period."

The silence was finally broken by my father asking for more information about the place. I painted a glowing picture for him. When I was finished, he said, "Well that sounds exciting. It will be a great experience for you. I'm not surprised you want to do this. Your grandmother went West in a covered wagon, you know. At least you won't have horses to contend with." He laughed warmly, and tears welled up in my eyes. Oh how I wanted to put my arms around him and hug him. How grateful I was for his understanding and confidence.

The entrance to a freeway brought me back to the present. Quickly I swung the pickup into the proper lane and followed the U-Haul with the Oregon license.

The rest of the day went smoothly, with regular stops to eat and go potty (drink 'em and drain 'em, as we called it when I taught first grade). About four o'clock we were coming into the Chicago area. "What a perfect time to arrive here," I groaned as the cars whizzed past me on both sides. I was having trouble going as slow as the U-Haul, whose maximum speed was fifty miles per hour. Finally I went around Tom's truck and felt better. Then I looked in the rearview mirror and couldn't see him. I had gotten too far ahead of him, and now we were separated. I worked my way over to the right-hand lane. There was no place to stop, so I went off the exit ramp. When I stopped at the end of the exit, I looked up at the overpass and saw Tom zooming past. When the light changed, I raced to the entrance ramp and got back on the freeway. I passed many cars trying to catch up with Tom. Then I saw him, not ahead of me, but in the oncoming lanes, heading in the direction from which we had just come.

"Oh no!" I yelled.

"What's wrong, Mommy?" Amy asked.

"Daddy's going the other way!" I shrieked. "What should I do now?"

The traffic was horrible, but I made my way to the right lane again. "If I get off again, he will probably just pass me again," I reasoned. "I guess I'd better just pull off and wait here until he comes past. I know he saw me because he waved his arm violently at me."

There was a stopping lane here, so I stopped. I waited and waited and waited. I didn't know it then, but Tom had stopped also and was waiting for me, thinking that I had turned around.

The longer I waited, the more I began to panic. I was in tears by the time a U-Haul truck came whizzing past. I checked the license, and sure enough they were Oregon tags. So I pulled out into the traffic as soon as I could manage it. I had to drive very fast to catch up with the truck.

"Why doesn't he slow down till I catch up?" I wanted to know. "And darn that car behind it. That woman won't let me get in behind the truck."

Finally I just pulled behind that car and decided I would have to follow that way. Then I saw a sign directing people to Toledo, and the truck took that lane. I followed obediently, but I was puzzled about why Tom would want to go back toward Ohio. I was too afraid to do anything but follow. Then we came to a toll gate. I began honking at the truck. The woman between us pulled over to another toll station, and I was finally behind the U-Haul. I honked again. Finally the door on the driver's side opened, and a man got out. It was not Tom!

I stared in pure shock as he walked toward me.

"You're not my husband," I screamed at him.

"No, lady, I'm not." He didn't seem sorry.

I began sobbing loudly. "You're not Tom. Where's Tom? Where am I?"

The lady in the toll station came out to me and tried to calm me down.

"Now the first thing we have to do is calm down," she instructed. She glanced at the cars lining up behind me. "Now where is your husband?"

"I don't know," I sobbed. "That's just it. I don't know."

"Okay. Okay," she said and began to pat my arm not too gently. "Now where are you supposed to be?"

"With him," I shrieked.

She took a deep breath and looked again at the traffic piling up behind us. "Where are you going?"

"To Washington."

"State or D.C.?"

"State."

"Okay. What you should do then is turn around here and go back to the (mumble) exit and head west. Maybe you can find him that way."

"All right," I agreed. I couldn't stay here, and I was willing to do anything.

The woman held up traffic till I turned around and started the other way. As I turned the pickup, I saw the man I'd thought was Tom talking with the woman who had been driving the car that wouldn't let me in. New tears came rolling down my face. "See, that's his wife. Where's my husband?"

I started down the freeway, looking at the exit signs.

"What one did she say, Amy? I don't remember."

Amy stared at me with very round eyes and didn't say a word.

In the next half hour I tried many exits. Tom was not waiting at any of them. My panic grew till I was unable to think clearly. At last I stopped at a filling station.

The attendant, a calm-looking, amiable black man, came out. I poured out my fears on him.

"Well what you should do is go back out on the freeway and go to the exit for I-90. Take that exit, and I bet you'll find him. That's the road west, and I'm sure you'll find him going that way."

"But what if I don't find him? I can't go on till I know where he is. What if I just go on and on and never find him at all?" And a fresh torrent of tears and sobs came.

"Okay, lady, take it easy. Pull on over there and park. There's a phone inside. Call the highway patrol. Maybe they know where he is."

I parked and went in the station. The phone would not work. Another attendant tried, but it just wouldn't work.

I went back to the black man. He looked irritated.

"Well, use the pay phone then."

I went to the pickup and searched the cab. My billfold was nowhere to be seen. Amy was on her knees, looking out the window. "Where's Daddy?" she asked.

That's just what I needed to hear!

"Where's Mommy's purse? Amy, have you seen Mommy's purse? Did you play with it?"

I had nightmarish visions of her throwing it out the window.

"No," she answered, "Sally."

Then I remembered. Sally did have it. I had given it to her at the last stop to buy a Coke.

"Oh no!" I groaned. "I don't have any money!"

I looked around. Everything looked foggy and smeary. My face felt crinkly from the dried tears. With a trembling hand I brushed away fresh tears. "I guess I'll just have to ask someone for a dime."

I started toward the black man. "What is it now, lady?" He was not enthusiastic about seeing me again.

I took a big, shaky breath. "Your phone inside doesn't work, and I don't have a dime. Would you please give me a dime to call the highway patrol?"

He looked at me as though he couldn't believe it. I must have looked like a wreck; I felt like one.

Shaking his head, he reached in his pocket and handed me a dime. Without a word he turned back to the gas pump.

"Thank you," I said quietly.

When I got hold of the highway patrol, I tried not to cry while I told the dispatcher my story. But I was unsuccessful in both categories. I had to repeat myself three times before it made any sense. Finally he told me to wait and he would check to see if Tom had called looking for me.

It seemed like hours before his strong, steady voice was in my ear again.

"Your husband has called, and he is at the Des Plaines Oasis. Now listen carefully, and I'll tell you how to get there. Are you listening?"

"Yes."

"Do you have anything to write on?"

"No."

"Just listen then." And he told me explicitly how to get where Tom was.

When he finished, he asked me to repeat the directions to him. I couldn't.

He told me again. I repeated what I could. My mind was in terrible shape. Finally I could say the directions correctly, but he had me repeat them twice more.

With dry eyes and trembling hands I pulled away from the gas station. Amy waved at the man, but he only shook his head and went inside the garage. Very carefully I followed the instructions of the patrolman, and to my great amazement I ended up at the Des Plaines Oasis. There was a U-Haul parked in the lot. Still I was not relieved until I saw it was really Tom who got out.

"Where have you been?" he demanded. Then taking a second

and closer look at me, his face softened, and he put his arms around me. New rushes of tears came, and between the sobs I tried to tell him what had happened. It was some time before we started out again. But this time I was obediently trailing behind the right U-Haul. I stayed there without exception for the rest of the seven-day trip to Chelan, Washington.

For the next six days we traveled over green hills, through cities, over vast, semiarid expanses, up mountains and down. They were uneventful days, and I was glad for that. While riding through the open and lovely vastness of Montana, my nerves began to heal, and I began to enjoy the trip. At last I was once again ready to anticipate our new home with excitement. The adventure once more became an adventure.

By late Wednesday afternoon our furniture and supplies were unloaded in the warehouse and waited to be put on the barge to travel the fifty-five miles to our new home. The four of us stood hand in hand at the edge of the lake.

As the sun slipped behind the mountains, a cool and gentle breeze began to blow. Amy and Sally tossed bread crumbs at the ducks paddling in the lake in front of us. Tom put his arms around me and pulled me close.

"This is our last night in the 'big world.' Tomorrow we'll be there." His voice was quiet as he looked up the lake twisting between the mountains. "Tomorrow we'll be in the wilderness."

One last struggle of doubt enveloped me, but the calmness, the beauty, and the quiet won. I was really glad to be going into the wilderness. It was the right thing for us. I sighed deeply and returned Tom's hug.

2

"Look at that big waterfall, Mommy," Sally shouted.

We were sitting on the outside deck of the *Lady of the Lake*, winding our way between the mountains, heading for Stehekin. The *Lady* is about sixty-four feet long, with a seating capacity on its two levels and outside deck of about one hundred fifty people. A magnificent waterfall tumbled into the lake from high above us. We had seen numerous waterfalls this morning, as well as a few deer grazing on the steep slopes.

As I leaned back and turned my face up to the sun, a feeling of contentment and quiet anticipation came over me. Except for the noise of the motor and occasional conversation among the passengers, the day was quiet and relaxed. Tom was feeling the peacefulness also.

"Not quite like Chicago, is it?" He grinned at me.

"Did you have to mention that?" I asked. It was still too fresh for me to laugh about it.

"Well at least you won't have traffic problems here," he said. "Course, there won't be a patrolman to help you out either."

"When are we going to get there?" Sally asked for the fiftieth time. Amy was sleeping on a bench.

"Soon."

"How long is soon?"

"About half an hour."

Thirty minutes later the Stehekin landing came into view. We could see a place for the boat to dock, a lodge, and a restaurant. There was a souvenir shop and a photo shop. On a hill to the right of these buildings was a large yellow lodge. We knew from our earlier visit that this was the old Golden West Lodge and was no longer being used. Farther to the right was a gray house. We had stayed there with the Wilsey family in March on the interview trip. To the left of the landing area one could see far into the valley, where the other residents lived scattered over nine miles. In the distance there were three mountain peaks, all sporting glaciers.

As we stepped off the boat, we were greeted by our former hosts. "Why look who's here. We thought you were coming tomorrow. Good to see you again. Welcome to the valley."

There were many introductions and offers of help, even a place to stay till our furniture came on tomorrow's barge. But we were eager to see our new home. We had seen it in March, but then it was totally covered with snow. We were anxious, after coming all this way, to see it and get moved in and settled.

After much discussion it was determined that Mr. Byrd, a valley resident and proprietor of the new shuttle bus service, would take us to our house in the new twelve-passenger van. He was hesitant, as were the other people with vehicles, to drive to where we lived. "We had a big flood over Memorial Day weekend, and it washed out the road that goes up that side of the valley. It's pretty rocky, but I s'pose we can make it."

We piled in, threw our gear in the back seat, and away we went. How beautiful it was as we wound along the edge of the lake and headed into the valley. We passed three occupied homes in three miles. Then we came to the schoolhouse. It did look different without all the snow around it. It was made of logs and was nestled among tall pines. The roof was steeply pitched to allow the snow to slide off. A sign announcing Stehekin School was nailed over the door.

"That's my school?" Sally asked in amazement.

"That's it!" said Tom. "Won't it be fun to go to school there?"

Sally didn't answer. She must have been thinking of the spacious brick building where she had just finished kindergarten.

We went around a curve and crossed a bubbling, full mountain creek. Within moments we were passing the most beautiful waterfall I'd ever seen. Last March it had been pretty, but now it was roaring as water fell 312 feet into a small pool that fed the creek we had just crossed.

"That's Rainbow Falls," Tom informed our girls.

They stared with round eyes and watched till it was out of view.

Another mile brought us to a fork in the road. Mr. Byrd took the left fork and crossed the river. Up to this point the road had not been too bad—dirt-packed, bumpy in spots, and narrow and twisty, but certainly not impassable. Once we crossed the bridge, the road began to deteriorate.

Bang! Rattle! Bounce! We jostled and jiggled with each revolution of the wheels. The rattling of the bus was roaring in our ears. We were the only passengers except for the driver's mother, who was posed quietly in the seat beside him. She seemed unaware of the heaving of the bus. She had lived in Stehekin many years, and I guessed that she was used to the roads.

After one big chuckhole a wail was added to the bedlam. Amy had banged her head on the side of the bus as it vaulted a boulder.

"This is quite a road," Tom shouted to Mr. Byrd, trying to make conversation.

"Oh it's pretty good here," Mr. Byrd hollered over his shoulder. "There's a couple places up a ways that are kinda bad." His straw hat hit the roof of the bus as we crawled over more rocks. My mop fell off the back seat.

Amy stopped crying to look at a deer poised beside the road. We were amazed to see it just standing there looking at us, but Mr. Byrd passed it with no more attention than I would have given a billboard last week. After we survived the rocky road, we glided along a dirt road. I saw giant ferns, and tall, lacy flowers wave as we swished by. McGregor Mountain came into view. I knew we were getting close to the house we had been assigned. I knew that McGregor, wearing its snowcap, would be my companion through the kitchen windows. I was elated. The beauty of the place! Pensive deer, flitting birds, billowing butterflies, awesome pines, racing creeks, jagged mountains. It was just as I had remembered and imagined.

Suddenly everything changed. The scenery was violated by an unsightly mess. Enormous, grotesque, rusty shapes lay along the road. Some monstrosities could be recognized as ancient vehicles. A rusted truck door leaned against a tree. A sink gleamed in the sun. All this junk must have been under the snow when we were here last March. I realized nine feet of snow could cover more than flowers and ferns. I began to feel uneasy. The snow had also covered the outside of our house up to the roof.

We passed a broken-down cabin, its roof sagging from the weight of many winters' snows. The back porch had collapsed. A door and a shovel rested against the side of the house. Moss grew on the gray, weathered log walls. An icebox, a broken rocker, and three wooden boxes were abandoned on the front porch. Cobwebs decorated the windows.

The bus went about fifty feet past the old cabin and stopped. "Here's the Olsons' house," Mr. Byrd announced as he parked in the middle of the road. He got out and opened the double side doors for us to get out. We stumbled out and stood in the road, aghast at this place. Our new home! Weeds and ferns grew four feet high all around the house. Windows were broken. Frayed wiring swayed in the breeze. Shakes were missing from the walls. A 1950 Chevy with a caved-in roof sat in the front yard next to a dilapidated shed.

As we stood immobilized by the sight, Mr. Byrd unloaded our things from the bus. He tipped his hat and got back in the driver's seat. As he drove away, his mother smiled kindly at us and waved. "Come see me if I can help you," she called.

Still we stood. The dust from the road blew over us: a man, a woman, two small girls, a box of cleaning supplies, a broom, a mop and bucket, a cooler of food, a suitcase of clothes, and three sleeping bags.

As the dust settled on the road again, Tom picked up the suitcase and walked slowly to the house. He stepped up on the wobbly concrete block that served as a step to the porch. The girls and I followed. Tom unlocked the door, and we stepped into the empty house and into our new life.

We wandered from room to room. The inside was as we remembered except for the broken windows. "The snow must have pushed them in," I thought as I surveyed the living room. It was large, with shelves on one wall and a huge stone fireplace opposite. The walls were real pine panels. There were three large windows.

I moved across the living room and into the kitchen. It was also large, with more cabinets than I'd ever had in any house. The big black cookstove stood on one side of the room. Opposite it were the windows looking out onto the river and McGregor Mountain. One of these windows was broken also.

I went back through the living room and into the hall. I found the girls in the front bedroom, which was to be theirs. Sally raced past me and into the bathroom.

"Mommy, Daddy, Amy, come look at this bathtub. It has turtle feet!" she squealed.

Sure enough, there sat the longest bathtub I'd ever seen. And it was perched on "turtle feet."

The back bedroom was inspected next. It was small but adequate for Tom and me. There were two windows looking out onto the river and mountain. The view more than made up for the smallness of the room.

We went back to the living room. I looked at Tom. The look of horror on his face had turned to dismay. His eyes questioned, "What do we do now?" Amy zipped between us, mopping the floor with the seat of her pants.

"Let's don't think," I suggested. "Let's just get busy cleaning before Amy does it for us."

We began washing the walls, closet, and floor in the girls' room. Then we scrubbed down the bathroom. By then we were no longer numb, just tired and hungry.

I went to the kitchen and had my first encounter with the stove. "How do I use you?" I asked it. Because it did not answer me, I began opening little compartments. "This must be the woodbox, where I build the fire. Now where's the wood?"

I found a small amount of wood out back, but it was in pieces too large for the stove.

"Tom, will you cut some wood so I can cook dinner?" I called to him.

"Okay," he said, and I heard the mop plop into the bucket in our bedroom. "I'll get the ax."

But he never moved.

"Lois," came his voice barely above a whisper, "the ax is in the pickup, and the—" His voice trailed off.

"And the pickup is in Chelan," I finished for him. "Now what do we do?"

"Mommy, come here quick. The toilet is spilling on the floor," Sally shouted from the bathroom.

I looked at Tom. I didn't know whether to laugh or cry. So I got the mop. Tom went to the front door and looked out. His back was to me, and I couldn't see his facial expression but I felt his confusion, disappointment, self-incrimination, and doubt. A wave of helplessness hit me. What could I do? I couldn't make dinner, and I didn't know how to help Tom. I looked at the mop in my hand and saw a stream of water starting down the hall. Well at least I can do something about that.

Just as I finished cleaning the bathroom for the second time that day, Tom shouted to us, "There's a pickup coming." And he raced out to the road.

Sally, Amy, the mop, and I were in the doorway when he came back.

"The man's going to the landing and said we could ride with him. Maybe we can eat at the restaurant."

I threw down the mop and pulled the door closed, glad to go away from the place for a while.

We rode the washboard road back toward the landing. About a mile before the landing we noticed a meadow filled with people and tables laden with food. Some of the people I recognized as having met last March; others were strangers to me. Most of the men wore baggy trousers and no shoes or shirts. Their hair was long, as were their beards. Many of the girls had long skirts, long hair, bare feet, and beautifully embroidered blouses.

"We call this the Hippie Meadow," our driver told us. "They invited the valley to a 'soul feast' tonight. You want to stop?"

"No. I think we'll just go on to the landing," Tom said.

So we did. We got out and thanked the driver, who was going on up the hill to a meeting. We climbed the steps to the restaurant, anticipating a meal. But instead we found the door locked and a sign saying CLOSED. A check with the hours and Tom's watch showed we were fifteen minutes too late to get dinner.

"Now what?" It seemed I'd already asked that question today.

"I'm hungry, Mommy," whined Amy, pulling on my leg.

"Let's go to McDonald's," suggested Sally.

"I know where there's some food," said Tom. "At the Hippie Meadow. I guess we could go back there."

"But it's too far to walk," I wailed.

"Yeh," he agreed. "But it isn't too far to the ranger station. I'll go up there and ask around if anyone is going that way. You stay here."

A few minutes later Tom came back driving a car.

"It's Darrell Wilsey's. He said his family is down at the meadow, and we can take the car to them. His wife will drive it back."

Shortly we were parking at the meadow. Ordinarily I would feel reluctant about crashing a party, especially when I didn't really know anyone there. But our desperate circumstances made us feel we were beyond etiquette. We walked up to the people and said simply, "We're hungry. May we eat with you?"

The man who seemed to be in charge smiled warmly at us. I barely saw the smile because I was fascinated with the bushy black hair caught up in a bun on the top of his head.

He was talking in a quiet, flowing sort of way and encouraged us to eat whatever we wanted and even take some home with us. One of the women brought us paper plates, and I began to circle the tables, looking for something familiar. Suddenly I wanted to laugh. How in the world had I gotten in this situation? Fifty feet from the table was a pen with chickens squawking and flying around; there was a compost heap nearby and a cabin hidden in the trees. Music from *Jesus Christ Superstar* was drifting out the windows. People were lying on the grass singly or in pairs and talking softly together.

Mitch, as the man introduced himself, spoke quietly behind me, offering to cut some chicken for us. He apologized that there was so little left. He said the chickens were small because they had been raised here. I accepted his meat and his smile with equal relief. I gave the girls some of the meat and some lemon jello. I found some fried fish under a bath towel. I suppose the towel was to keep the fish warm, but who knows; I was beyond shock. There was a salad of strange-looking weeds and flowers. I passed it by. There were peanut butter cookies, which the girls were delighted to see. There was lots of homemade wheat bread that was very delicious. We sat on the grass and ate, declining the home brew and choosing Kool-Aid instead. Most of the people came over to us and welcomed us warmly. I was beginning to feel much better about everything when I realized we were six miles from home.

"How do we get home?" I whispered to Tom.

He didn't answer. He just kept chewing on the tiny chicken leg and shrugged his shoulders.

When the party broke up, we found ourselves headed up the road toward home, although it was hard to think of it as such. We were riding in an ancient VW with the teacher whom Tom was replacing. My bones were too far gone to respond to the beating they took. My mind was blank. Sally stared blankly out the window. Amy sat quietly on Tom's lap. On my lap sat a seeping lemon meringue pie. Somehow my last trick for the day was to keep that pie from slopping over while we crawled over one rock after another in that tiny car.

None of us minded sleeping on the floor that night. We were just glad to be still. My body was exhausted, but my mind continued to work. I had not had a relationship with God since my childhood days. He had been very real to me then as He strengthened me and got me through my long illness due to polio. But in my college days I had forgotten Him, I had been able to handle everything by myself. But as I lay on the floor that first night in Stehekin, I knew I would not be able to handle this by myself. A short, simple prayer formed in my mind: "Thank You, God, that this day is over. Please help me through tomorrow."

3

I woke with two distinct sensations. My back was stiff all over from lying on the floor all night, and I heard a popping, crackly sound. I sat up. Tom's sleeping bag was empty. The crackling sound came from the kitchen, and a smoky smell confirmed my guess. Tom had a fire going.

"Where'd you get the wood?" I asked him from the kitchen door.

Tom's relaxed smile preceded his explanation. "I got up this morning and walked to the Byrd's cabin and borrowed their ax," he said proudly.

"Why didn't we think of that yesterday?" I asked. "Oh well, I'm proud of you for thinking of it this morning." I gave him a big hug.

He gathered me in his arms. "Things will be better today," he promised. "We'll get our furniture and boxes from the barge, and we can start to get settled."

We walked to the window and stood looking at the rushing river and the snowcapped McGregor. A doe wandered out of the woods, and as we watched, she made her way to the edge of the river. She looked cautiously around before bending her head to drink. Just then a tiny, bright flash zipped by the window. It was back in an instant, staring at us through the broken glass. It was a hummingbird, his ruby throat sparkling as though it was covered with sequins. I was so startled I held my breath. In an instant he was gone.

"I knew there was a reason I wanted to come here," I said to

Tom. "I forgot it yesterday, but maybe I'll be able to remember it today."

But the tests weren't over yet.

The one-o'clock arrival of the barge found us waiting on the dock. We watched as the barge approached, plowing through the waves, sending great splashes of water over the open deck. I was thankful for the tarps that covered most of the things, but I still wondered if my treasures were staying dry. As the barge came closer, I had another surprise. Yes, there were our packing boxes, our pickup, and some pieces of furniture. But there were also lumber and other building supplies, a goat, four horses, and some hay. It was a good thing my material heart had already been broken; otherwise I could not have survived my maple dining room table next to livestock.

We began the numerous trips back and forth to our house. It was a slow process because our pickup did not hold much at one time. The creek-bed road was also a factor in the slowness of the project. One of the school board members and a young man helped by taking a couple of loads for us.

When we got it all home, we had an odd assortment. Mattress for one bed and springs for another, a tabletop but no legs, the Hide-A-Bed with cushions missing, and so on. There had not been room for everything on this barge.

Four days later the barge returned with the rest of our things, along with a road grader, a jeep, and one hundred bales of hay. Everything seemed to be there and in amazingly good shape, considering the cross-country U-Haul journey, a few days in a warehouse, a water-sprayed barge trip with livestock, and a seven-mile trip in a pickup over creek-bed roads. We were missing only one thing, a case of toilet paper. Here was a real problem. We considered this to be a necessary item, and we were in definite need. Mrs. Byrd had loaned us one roll, and it was nearly gone. But how does one go about asking in a new community if anyone has seen one's toilet paper?

The next time we were at the landing, I walked into the lodge restaurant and coffee shop. The screen door banged behind me. I looked around to decide where to sit. To my left was the dining room, with its paneled walls, big windows facing the lake, stone fireplace with crossed snowshoes hanging above it, and several small tables with red and white checked cloths and wooden chairs pulled up. That room looked very inviting, but no one was there who could help me. So I sat down at the counter of the coffee shop. This place, along with the store–post office, was the hub of the landing and valley activity. But I felt very strange sitting at a coffee shop counter working up my courage to ask if anyone had seen my toilet paper.

Too soon someone came to ask if they could help me. No I didn't want coffee. Yes the pie looked very good, but I really wasn't hungry. Finally I blurted it out.

"I'm Lois Olson, the new teacher's wife. Ah—we—ah—brought a lot of supplies in with us, and everything seems to have made it except"—I looked down at the counter—"our case of toilet paper."

I looked up at the shocked face.

"A case of toilet paper?" The shock was changing very quickly into a swallowed snort, then finally into a full-blown roar of laughter.

I wanted to get under the stool, but because there was no room, I began to smile and nod my head in a silly sort of way. This was so ridiculous!

The person's laughter drew some other workers, and they were informed in gasps that the Olsons had lost their toilet paper.

Finally some kind soul went to look in the lodge storeroom. It was possible that the case was thought to have belonged to the lodge. It was unbelievable that anyone else would buy a whole case. At this point I not only wished I'd never bought it, but I wished I'd never asked for it back! What a way to be introduced to valley life! The person mercifully returned with my lost article. I was more than glad to take the errant box, with its ridiculous contents, and escape to the car.

For the next couple of weeks we worked at getting the house unpacked and arranged. Tom also had to spend some time cutting wood for the stove. His twenty-minute lesson in Ohio from the man who sold him the saw proved to be very inadequate.

We were shown a very large downed tree we could cut up for

firewood. It was located in an open area that had once been intended to be a fairway of a golf course. The course and its lodge never existed outside the dream of their creator. Some work had been done clearing areas for fairways, but that was about all that was accomplished. The tree we began to work on was one of the few that had not rotted beyond use.

We drove the truck in as far as possible and then tramped through the knee-high grass. Sally, who had a very active imagination, played around the area with Amy and their make-believe companions. I watched as Tom cut through the large trunk with the saw. I felt some of his tension but knew even less about the whole thing than he did. I was willing to fetch and carry, but that was the extent of my helping ability.

One morning he went off to cut wood by himself while I worked at home. In a short while he returned. His eyes flashed with anger and frustration.

"A screw came out of the saw! Can you believe it? One little screw is gone, and I can't use the saw! I looked all over for it, but you know how tall that grass is. I may as well look for a needle in a haystack!"

He stormed to the back porch and the toolbox. A thorough and noisy search did not produce a screw of the necessary size. Every screw was either a little too big or a fraction too small.

The thought occurred to me to go ask someone for a screw, but after the toilet paper incident I was very shy to reveal any more of our problems and inadequacies. Tom must have had the same thought because he stood up holding a magnet.

"Let's go look for the screw with this."

Sally and Amy crawled through the grass and found everything but a screw. Tom and I looked with the magnet and were equally unsuccessful. A stormy cloud rode with us back home. The next mail carried a letter to the hardware store in Chelan asking for *ten* screws of this exact size for the saw!

The woodcutting went on with moderate increase in skill. One noon shortly after the lost screw ordeal Tom came home from cutting with a companion. It was Mitch, the strange-looking but very pleasant man who had served us at the soul feast. He came in with a warmth and friendliness that puzzled me. He was so weird-looking. How could he be so nice, too? Nice people were supposed to look, well, not like this anyway.

Mitch looked around through the house (I thought that was strange, to just go looking everywhere in someone's home when you really didn't even know the people), and he remarked over the possibility of the porch being a good place to raise potatoes in cardboard boxes. I had been so stunned as I followed his black bushy bun through my house that his talking about raising potatoes in cardboard boxes seemed just the thing I should do this fall.

When he and Tom left with the tool they had come home to get, I had agreed we'd come to the Hippie Meadow for dinner the next evening. As he said, "Why not? The garden is producing, and the goat is fresh, so why not?"

"What time would you like us to come?" I asked.

He smiled and shrugged his shoulders. "What time? Who cares? Come when you want."

I had spent thirty years in the city and only three weeks in the "freedom" of the Stehekin Valley. I had not yet shed the control of clocks.

"How 'bout if we come at seven o'clock?" I suggested.

"Suit yourself." His hands reached shoulder height with palms up, and he followed Tom to our truck.

As I watched them disappear, I wondered what he meant by "the goat is fresh." Surely we would not be eating goat meat! But on the other hand, considering, well—gosh. Maybe I shouldn't have said we'd come.

Because the meadow was nearly marsh, I put overalls and long-sleeve shirts on Sally and Amy to protect them from the mosquitoes. At six forty-five we arrived at the meadow. As we doused ourselves with 6-12, Mitch came running out from behind some trees, waving warmly.

I looked around the meadow with more clarity than I had the first time we were there. It was a large field bordered on one side by the road, on another side by marsh, and on the remaining two sides by woods and mountains. The field had a garden fenced with logs and wires. There was a large fenced area with chickens squawking and flitting around. Another enclosure had rabbits as prisoners. The fences were partly boards and partly logs and wires. A utility pole supported electrical wires to this point, and had a refrigerator tied to it. Three goats were tied to three separate trees. Hidden in the woods were an assortment of buildings with a maze of paths connecting them. None of the cabins had water or electricity, and no one seemed to mind.

We stood in the meadow for a while, making faltering conversation. Then Mitch took Sally and Amy on a tour of the livestock. I was beginning to think I had dreamed up the dinner invitation. Finally Mitch muttered something about Lenore, his wife, being at the house making dinner. That encouraged us because we were getting hungry.

After the livestock tour Mitch led us down a muddy path into the woods and stopped in front of a house. The cabin looked to be one room, about ten feet by twelve feet. It had been built with scraps. None of the windows matched. The boards were of various woods and colors. The door had obviously hung in another house. I saw a bushy head moving around inside and assumed it was Lenore preparing dinner. After deciding I should not go into the cabin because no one had asked me, I turned my attention back to Mitch's monologue and watched him hammer a couple of upright boards into a wooden box. He was making a milking stand for Gypsie to make milking time a little more pleasant.

"The goat's head will go between these boards, and a bowl of oats will sit on this box," he explained. To keep the front end busy while he worked on the back end, I surmised.

I shifted the kids' jackets to my left arm so I could swat at a mosquito, but the slap was ineffective because my hand was getting numb from holding frozen hamburger I had brought along as a gift for the hostess.

Mitch began talking about how he was making shakes out of cedar. He was planning to put them on the house. I glanced at the house. It already had shakes. Then I realized this must not be his house. Who, then, was wandering around inside?

A cat slunk around the corner of the house and gave us a sideways glare. Then he ambled over to a bowl of foul-looking stuff and began to eat. Amy darted toward him. Mitch stood up quickly.

"Um"—he paused—"that's Cougar Cat, and he doesn't care to be petted," he finished quickly.

I nearly dropped the jackets and meat in my attempt to catch Amy before she got to the cat. Tom reached her just in time to avert disaster.

The commotion aroused the bushy-haired person. As the door opened slowly and I prepared to greet a fellow housewife, my smile froze. A six-foot, four-inch man stepped over the raised threshold. His peace beads swung out away from his body as he bent to get out the door.

I stared in bewilderment as Mitch explained, "This is Jacob." And that's all the introduction we had. Mitch went back to his handiwork. Nothing else was said.

My stomach took a dive in despair.

Eventually Jacob announced that he was going to get some berries and wandered away into the woods swinging a dirty, cracked Pyrex mixing bowl.

Mitch stood up and silently admired his work.

"Are you going to milk the goat now?" I asked, just to make sure I could still speak.

"After I sterilize the things," he answered. "Come with me." He picked up the box-and-boards milking stand and started off farther into the woods.

Sally began complaining that her stomach hurt. I knew she was hungry because we usually ate at six-thirty, but she thought she had to go potty. My heart sank at the thought, but I took her a few steps to the outhouse, calling to Tom to wait because I was sure I would get lost if he left me there. The journey halted while Sally tried to go potty.

The door to the outhouse was held closed by a big rock. That meant I had to move it with my hands. I looked around to find a place to put down the jackets and the frozen meat, but there was only mud and trees. I tried to kick the stone away from the door but only hurt my toe. Sally began to whimper. I looked around desperately and decided that the old stump wasn't so bad after all.

I put the stuff down, moved the stone, and opened the door, wondering what I would see or smell.

It was very clean, but the hole was right on the ground and surrounded by smooth wood. Sally hesitated as I undid her overalls. After all this I thought she should go potty. She tried, but she really didn't want to sit on the boards, and she couldn't go standing up. We fastened her up, put down the wooden lid, closed the door, pushed the stone back in place, and picked up the jackets and meat. We had to hurry to keep up with Tom and Mitch and Amy.

Mitch stopped trotting long enough to ask if we would like to have some wine he had made. I didn't want any, especially with my stomach so empty, but didn't want to offend Mitch. I muttered something about having it with dinner and not wanting to bother him now, with the milking to do and all.

"It's no bother," he hollered over his shoulder as he ran down the path. "It's just here in the freezer."

Freezer? "Here, take this meat I brought for you." I had to shout for him to return. "I wanted to bring you something. I know how hard it is to get meat up here," my voice trailed off in my attempt to explain. A package of frozen meat seemed rather ridiculous right then. It suddenly occurred to me that he was probably a vegetarian anyway.

"Thank you." And he was gone, dissolved into the woods.

I looked at Tom. He looked as skeptical as I felt.

"Let's go up to the house to drink the wine," Mitch called, reappearing on the path.

I silently agreed. I'd rather pass out in a chair than in the woods. We trudged up the path past a small A-frame cabin and into another cabin, which belonged to a friend of Mitch's.

Inside the plank front door the floor was uneven stone and concrete. The walls were made of flat spools of wood set in concrete. Stepping up onto the wood floor of the living room, I tried to decide where to sit down. There was a black horsehair-looking couch, a huge, heavily carved rocking chair, and a straight chair. Tom headed for the rocker. I decided the couch would be too scratchy and probably had bugs, too, so I sat on the straight chair, which creaked and groaned. Sally and Amy sat on the edge of the couch. From my perch I squinted to see the back of the house and was amazed to see it had a dirt floor. A ladder led to the sleeping area upstairs.

Mitch, meanwhile, rummaged around in the dirty dishes on the counter and finally came up with three wineglasses. After swishing them in a bucket of water and shaking them twice, he cleared an open space on the bar with a sweep of his arm and set the glasses down.

He uncorked the green bottle and held it up to read the label. "This is cherry wine," he announced, and poured it into the glasses.

I gulped and mumbled agreement to his toast, swallowing some wine with a silent prayer. The wine was amazingly good. While I was trying to see if it had anything floating around in it without appearing to be looking for floating objects, the door banged open. One of the legs separated from the rung of my chair when I jumped.

"This is Lenore," was Mitch's introduction.

Lenore was small and pretty. She had a long black braid down her back. A yellow T-shirt clung to a very shapely torso that was quite mobile because it was unhampered by a bra. Her trousers, held up by a drawstring, were bright blue with red flowers. Tennis shoes completed the outfit.

"I've been berrypicking," she said. My visions of dinner faded beyond recognition. As she wandered around the kitchen, looking over the dirty dishes, apparently in search of a glass, Mitch distracted her. "I think you should milk Gypsie tonight. You get more milk from her than I do."

"Okay," she acquiesced.

Mitch decided he would "pick a salad" and invited us to go with him.

"I'd like to watch Lenore milk the goat if she doesn't mind," I said.

Mitch shrugged. "Choose your activity."

Tom and Amy went to pick a salad. Sally and I stayed behind. After I downed the wine, we went outside again, where a kettle of boiling water steamed on a propane stove. Lenore put some of the water in a large bowl and swished it around several times. I watched until the wine and my empty stomach made me dizzy. Finally she dumped the water on the ground, sat the bowl down, poured more hot water into a smaller bowl, and added a squirt of liquid detergent. More water was put into a tin coffeepot. In the meantime she asked Sally what her name was. When Sally told her, she replied, "That's a pretty name." She finished her work in silence.

Lenore picked up the coffeepot and a clean dish towel. She gave me the bowl with the soap in it. Sally got the large bowl to carry. "Don't put your fingers in it," she cautioned. We followed Lenore as quickly as we could, but she got to the meadow long before we did.

Tom, Amy, and Mitch were already in the meadow, with the empty salad bowl in the grass. Mitch had untied the goat and was bringing her toward us.

"Put the things down by the gate," Lenore said to us as she pointed at the chicken pen. She went to help Mitch direct Gypsie, who was pulling in the opposite direction, to the gate. Her udder was so enlarged with milk that she tripped over it.

Mitch left the goat with Lenore and went into the chicken pen to chase the chickens out of the area where they milked the goat. He wasn't very successful, so Tom and Amy went in, too. Tom looked comical chasing chickens around the pen, waving his arms and hollering. One chicken flew at Amy. She screamed. Tom continued chasing chickens and hollering, but now he was carrying Amy, too.

My stomach growled. It was seven thirty-five.

The milking was highly unsuccessful. Gypsie did not care for her new milking stand and quickly pulled away from it. She stepped in the "sterile" bowl of milk.

"Drat!" was not Lenore's comment as she ducked out of the way of the rebellious goat.

In muffled tones Mitch persuaded Lenore to dump the milk. She did so, unwillingly. They tried again. This time Gypsie not only dumped the bowl but pulled Mitch under the lograiling around the milking stand and dragged him around the chicken pen.

Jacob appeared again. "Shades of *Animal Farm*." He chuckled and stayed to watch.

After several more attempts at milking Lenore decided the spectators should go back to the house and wait while they did the milking.

Mitch hollered to Jacob to pick a salad, but he silently continued into the woods. The empty salad bowl lay abandoned in the grass. Jacob turned off onto one of the paths before we got to the house. Tom, the girls, and I sat quietly in the darkening, empty house, our stomachs grumbling in unison. It was eight o'clock.

After another ten minutes people began to appear, some of whom we had seen before and some we had not. When Mitch and Lenore came back with no milk, I was glad. I didn't want to drink any after seeing Gypsie step in the bowl.

Lenore collapsed on the couch. "Mitch, that milking stand was about strong enough for Cougar Cat," she reproached him quietly. "We have to remember what we're working with."

They were silent for a while.

"I think goats are like children," Lenore continued as if she hadn't paused. "You have to let them know who's in charge."

That seemed to decide the dilemma for her. She got up and went back to the kitchen. Mitch did his hands-up gesture and followed her.

My girls watched quietly as confusion reigned. Debbie washed dishes and everyone else talked and laughed and hugged and kissed. We were offered more wine but declined.

Tom and I looked on as Mitch made something with eggs, beating them ferociously. Debbie began some peanut butter balls. Lenore asked Debbie why she was wearing a bra.

"It's not a bra. It's my bathing suit!" Debbie replied defensively.

Lenore then decided to make a salad dressing. Lemon juice was the only ingredient I recognized. Someone finally arrived with a bowl of leaves and flowers for salad and then Mitch disappeared outside with his bowl of whatever-it-was. More people came and went, banging the plank door. I had long ago stopped jumping with the bangs. The chair couldn't take it. During all this it had been getting very dark, but no one seemed to notice except us. Tom's stomach began to roar.

Mitch finally returned with the announcement that he was making crepes, and did we want ours with cheese or berries? By this time even crepes sounded good. Evidently they were edible, because he was offering them with cheese or berries. We decided on cheese. He lit a kerosene lantern, pushed aside some things on the bar, put the lantern down, and left again.

Someone offered us a burnt peanut butter cookie. We took it.

By eight thirty-five Mitch returned with a plate of food. He handed it to Sally and left again. Sally looked at it, squinting in the dim light. It looked like a rolled-up pancake with cheese inside it. Heaped beside it was something not quite rice and not quite hominy. Sally sighed and asked for a drink of water. I fished around in the rubble and found one of the wineglasses we had used. Someone dipped it into a bucket and handed it to me. I took it as if I always drank water from a bucket shared by the multitudes. I turned and stumbled over the step up to the living room.

Then Mitch returned with a plate for Amy, which I shared with her. The crepes were pretty good, made with whole wheat flour. The other stuff was atrocious. After everyone had been served and was sitting around on the living room floor, we found out the ricelike stuff was kasha, or buckwheat groats. We couldn't eat it. We ate the salad without dressing, drank as little water as possible, talked when we could, and laughed when we couldn't.

At nine o'clock someone announced the Charlie Chaplin movies were beginning at the community hall. It cost a quarter if you had money. They were being shown in an effort to raise money to pay for the new wiring in the hall. Tom seized the idea. We couldn't go to the movies because the girls needed to go to bed, but we would be happy to drive the others to the hall because we passed it on our way home.

We left the house in the same shambles it had been in when we came. People jumped into the back of the pickup, and we started down the rocky, dusty road just as the moon appeared over the mountains. Mitch waved to us from the meadow grass, where he was reclining and eating salad with chopsticks.

Later, as I was bathing Sally and Amy in the long tub with the turtle feet, Sally said with great relief in her voice, "Mama, I'm glad we have a potty that's a potty."

I smiled in genuine agreement. "Me, too, Sweetie. Me, too."

After a snack of fruit and cookies we put the girls to bed. I washed the few dishes with vigor and then sat down beside Tom on the couch. He was looking into the fire. I moved close to him. I wanted to talk about the evening.

"Would you like groats for breakfast?" I asked. I meant it to be funny because I wasn't sure how to talk about our recent experience.

"No thank you," he said and turned to look in my eyes. "Sweetie Pie, we're in for a lot of growing."

I looked away from him into the fire. I was a little frightened by the whole thing. I put my arm under his and took his hand. "I'm glad I don't have to do it without you."

I looked into his eyes again and saw that he was not at all sure he would be any security for me. "I'm glad I don't have to do it without you," he replied.

A picture flashed through my mind of our wedding day. Because of college we had been engaged for nearly three years before we got married. We were both so excited when we stood at last at the altar of the chapel. A profound feeling of joining ourselves together enveloped us at that moment. In the cabin, in front of the fire, we were once again stating our need for each other and pledging ourselves to help and love each other for better or for worse. There was a distinct possibility that vow would be tested and strengthened in this new life we'd chosen.

Once more a simple prayer formed in my mind: "God, help us."

4

As we began to settle in our house, we found that we were not the only residents. Many generations of field mice had occupied the place, and they were not eager to share it with us. At first I didn't mind them too much; they were so cute and tiny. They were a nuisance but tolerable.

One night Tom and I were sitting cozily in front of the fire. He was in the leather chair reading, and I was on the couch with a very interesting book on the ferns of the area. I was just at the exciting part that told about the ferns' reproductive systems when a mouse walked up the back of the couch, over my shoulder, down the front of me, and finally onto the floor. With a very uncountrified screech I jumped off the couch and into Tom's lap. When he stopped laughing and I stopped screeching, we decided the War of the Mice had to begin immediately. It did. For many days it was uncertain who would win. We had all sorts of traps set. We did not want to use poison because we were sure Amy would be the only one to sample it.

One valley person told us how to make a water trap. We were getting desperate, so we tried it. We filled a bucket with water, strung a can smeared with peanut butter across the top of the bucket, and leaned a piece of wood against the bucket as a ramp for the mice. That night I was awakened by a splashing sound. Sure enough, a mouse had run up the wood to get to the peanut butter and had fallen into the water. "One more for our side," I said proudly. But before the night was over, I was determined not to use that trap again. That mouse treaded water all night, and I had to listen to his frantic splashing.

It was about this same time that we discovered there was an "upstairs family." They were a very busy family as well as very noisy. No doubt we disturbed them in the daytime because they certainly disturbed us at night. Such thumping and banging I'd never heard. Many a night we woke with a start after some loud crash in the attic. In the pitch-black night I would hear a little voice from the other bedroom saying, "Mama, what was that? It scares me."

I dared not say back, "It scares me, too. I wonder if it's an earthly creature or otherwise." Instead I'd say, "It's just the family that lives upstairs. Don't worry."

"But, Mama, what if the family upstairs comes downstairs?"

"She wonders that, too," I thought. "Well if they come downstairs, we will be very nice to them and invite them for tea and cookies." It was a very silly answer, but I didn't know what else to say.

It wasn't long before the upstairs family did come downstairs. They came only at night and made raids through the house. We began missing little things such as barrettes and safety pins. The rag rug in the bathroom began to disappear piece by piece.

"Maybe it's the Borrowers, Mama," suggested Sally. Because we had no television, I read to the girls every night. We had recently read a book about the Borrowers, who lived in people's walls and borrowed things to use in their own little houses in the walls.

The next nightly banging session produced a little voice from the other bedroom. "Mama, I don't think it's the Borrowers. It makes too much noise for little people."

That same night the upstairs creatures knocked our wineglasses off the kitchen counter.

"That's it!" I shrieked. "They've gone too far. I'm getting a trap!"

We borrowed a live-animal trap and baited it with peanut butter. About five o'clock the next morning I was awakened by the sound of the trap's doors clanging shut.

"We got him, Tom," I whispered loudly, shaking him.

"What? We got what?" came the groggy voice.

"Him. I just heard the trap go off."

"Oh. Why don't you go see what it is?" he said as he rolled over to get comfortable again.

"By myself?" It was incredible.

"Sure. Why not?"

After a few more words we both tiptoed into the kitchen and flipped on the light. The cage was filled with a very bushy animal, gray and furry like a squirrel. I looked at the face and gasped. It was a rat! A rat—right there in my kitchen! There were rats living upstairs! Rats walking on my kitchen counters! Rats taking pieces out of my rug! Why, they could even have been in my bedroom while I was asleep! They could even have gotten on my bed!

I had to sit down.

"A bushy-tailed wood rat," Tom said quietly. "A pack rat." He began to laugh.

"How can you laugh? I think it's perfectly horrid!"

"It is, but it's funny, too. Think of all the things we thought of when we heard those noises, and all the time it was this rat." He began to laugh again.

I began to cry. "What if there are more upstairs? I can't stand to live in a house with rats. I won't!"

Tom stopped laughing and put his arms around me. "Remember when we were first married and we found a roach in our bed? We took care of it, didn't we? We'll take care of this problem, too. Maybe this is the only one. These things aren't very sociable. Say, you're shaking. Let me get a fire going, and then I'll take him out of here."

That night I lay awake, staring into the blackness and straining my ears to hear a noise that meant there were more rats in the house. But the upstairs noises stopped, and the bathroom rug stopped shrinking. (We lost the "bathroom curtains" to a bear, though. My mother was horrified when I wrote that sentence to her. Later I told her that our bathroom curtain was an elderberry bush outside the bathroom window and that a bear came one night and ate the berries and trampled down the bush.)

With the victory of the Mouse War seeming certain, and the

upstairs family taken care of, and the broken windows fixed, and
the frayed wiring repaired, and new screens that Tom's father had
brought for us on his parents' first visit installed, I began to feel
better about our home. Tom got a part-time job driving the shuttle bus, and in off-hours he and I worked at cutting down the jun-
gle of ferns that surrounded the house.

Another of my frustrations—my frustration with the stove—
began to work out. I had cooked on a wood-burning stove when
we lived three months in the tenthouse in Yosemite National
Park. It had been a very interesting experience then, but I had
never learned to bake anything. Whatever I put in the oven came
out a black, charred, unedible blob. This stove was a much nicer
one, and I was determined to learn to use it. I had to. There really
was no alternative; one cannot make everything on top of the
stove. I had to bake six loaves of bread a week, so the stove and I
had to learn to work together. At first I would forget to add more
wood, and the fire would nearly go out. Then I would build it
back up and get it too hot. Gradually I learned how much wood
was necessary to keep an even heat flow. I also learned to turn
what I was baking because the side closest to the woodbox cooked
faster than the other side. Our bread was no longer doughy but
light on the inside and golden-crusted on the outside. I was very
proud. I learned to bake juicy, golden brown pies, and cookies
were a snap. Meat loaf and other baked meats were fine if I allowed enough time. Cakes were my only failure. I never learned to
bake a cake in that oven. Every time I turned a cake, it would fall.
We ate many sorts of "brownies" before I gave up on cakes.

I began to enjoy the stove. The warmth it gave on a chilly
morning was so friendly, and the aroma of the wood burning and
the noise of it snapping and popping provided company for me in
the empty kitchen before the rest of the family were up and
about.

There is something very tender about seeing little tousle-headed
children in their footed blanket sleepers patter sleepy-eyed into
the kitchen and pull a little chair up to the stove.

The warming ovens above the stovetop were very handy and
kept foods at just the right temperature. A cooled pie placed in

the warming ovens while dinner cooked would be just warmed through by dessert time. Canned vegetables could be heated right in the opened can on top of the stove. Food set over the woodbox would boil rapidly, and food set on the opposite side of the top would simmer quietly. I began to find a joy and pride in my cooking that I had not had since Tom and I were first married. The fresh air and much outdoor exercise gave us hearty appetites, and it was a pleasure to satisfy it with the products from the stove.

The stove also helped us to cultivate one of our first friendships. Karl was a little boy who lived nearby. He was a second grader and would, of course, be one of Tom's students. Karl was very pleasant and obviously liked to eat. Any time Karl was aware that I was baking cookies, he was more than happy to carry wood in for me in exchange for samples from the oven. I enjoyed the times Karl spent with us in the kitchen. He seemed interested in us and no doubt marveled at the way I did things in comparison with his mother. Rhoda had lived in the valley for years and was most adept at meeting the demands this kind of living placed on women. There were times when Karl seemed to feel my actions were unnecessary. Once he came over when I was washing the windows.

"What are you doing that for?" he asked. "The birds will just fly into them."

He was right. I stopped cleaning them so often.

Karl and Sally played together on occasion. Sally was not quite sure at first about Karl and the things he liked to do. Karl loved to play in the dirt with trucks and road graders. He was mechanically gifted and loved to putter with machines. Sally wasn't sure how to play with him because she didn't particularly like trucks and road graders and machines, and she just couldn't throw off her city upbringing that dictated a very strict cleanliness code. Sally just could not roll in the dirt. They did, however, have good times together. They played a modified version of house because Karl was not inclined to that sort of play. They hunted bears in the tall ferns, and Sally cooked up amazing brews of weeds and flowers. They collected rocks and displayed them on the side of the road and tried to convince the tourists that came by in the shuttle bus to buy the rocks. That was one trap that never caught a tourist.

Sally often rode her bike up to the Byrd's cabin. She loved going to the "Byrd House," as she called it. She spent many lovely hours with "Grandma" Byrd. They went to the river and fetched water in buckets together. They picked berries and made them into pies, with Sally standing on the flour box to reach the table-top. Grandma Byrd told stories of her childhood and taught Sally beautiful little songs. Grandma Byrd was to become a cherished friend of our whole family.

As things at home became a little more routine, the girls and I liked to go on hikes while Tom was driving the shuttle bus. At first we wandered up and down the road. We found all sorts of things hiding in the ferns and woods: old cars, rusted tools, ice-boxes, and even summer cottages down little, overgrown road tracks. Some cottages appeared to have been used recently, and others looked as though they had been abandoned for some time.

After we had explored our area to our satisfaction, we decided to ride to the landing with Tom and walk a ways on the Lake Shore Trail. It was said to be an easy trail as well as a scenic one. It followed along the lakeshore for seventeen miles. Of course we could go as far as we liked and turn around. The first time the girls and I hiked along that trail, I was rather apprehensive. We were definitely alone, and for all my apparent ease in tramping the woods, I really was unsure of what we might find and what I would do with two little girls if in fact we did meet a wild animal. Sally skipped ahead, and Amy half ran, half walked in her usual way, trying to keep up with Sally and do everything Sally did. It was fine except when the trail was very narrow and there was a drop-off on the side into the lake. I nervously held Amy's hand along these places. I kept my eyes and ears open for any sugges-tion that we were not the only ones in the woods. In the open areas I could relax more and enjoy the magnificent view of lake and mountains.

Then it happened. We were going along a narrow, high place in the trail with a rock ledge right next to us.

"Hold Mama's hand, Amy. Watch where you are going. That's a girl."

Our concentration was broken by a rustling sound on the rock ledge above us. I froze, but my heart began to race. I was afraid to look up. I was sure I would see a bear looking down at us. I looked at Sally. She seemed to have heard the noise, and seeing the fear on my face, she looked puzzled.

"What's wrong, Mama?" she asked.

"Did you hear that noise?"

"Yes. There it is again."

I began to chastize myself silently. "How silly you are to bring these little girls into the wild woods! Really, you should have known better. Think of all the stories you've heard about bears."

My thoughts were interrupted by Sally's squeal of delight. "Look, Mama. There's the thing that's making the noises." Fearfully I followed her pointing hand. There above us on the rock ledge sat a chipmunk!

"Isn't he cute? Look, Amy," Sally was saying. "See that little animal. It's a chipmunk."

Amy stared in delight as she said in her two-year-old way, "Chipmunk." She watched it foraging in the pine duff and leaves and said, "Get it, Sally. Get it for Amy."

I sighed with the release of my anxiety and had to laugh at myself. All that fright over a chipmunk! What a nature girl I was! I would certainly have to improve on this score.

Another outing proved to be more successful. It was our first berrypicking trip later in the summer, when the berries were ripe. Karl told us where we might find some blackcaps, so we decided to take a look. The sun was hot during the main part of the day, so we decided to go early one morning after Tom left for work.

I stood in the doorway of the girls' room and watched as they were awakened by the sun streaming on their faces. Sally sat up slowly and brushed back the hair that had fallen in her eyes. Amy drowsily looked around for her Blankie. She found it on the floor beside her bed.

"Hi, Mama," Sally said as she blinked sleepily at me. "The sun's awake."

"Good morning, girls," I said as I hugged them.

"Did you have a nice sleep?" Amy asked her usual morning question.

"I sure did. Did you?"

"Ah huh."

Sally nodded her head.

"Good," I said, "because I need two big girls with lots of energy to help me this morning."

"Doing what?" Sally asked.

"Picking blackberries," I said. "Karl says there should be some near the airstrip just about ripe for picking."

"Hooray," shouted Sally, and she began dancing around the room.

Amy was a bit puzzled by Sally's reaction. She hadn't been berrypicking and didn't know what it was all about. She watched Sally a minute and then jumped off the bed and began dancing and hollering, too. I guess she decided that if Sally thought berrypicking was fun, then it must be. She and Blankie whirled until they dropped with dizziness.

I took their clothes out of the closet and said, "Okay, now. You girls get dressed while I make your beds. You better wear these long pants so the berry thorns won't scratch your legs."

Sally usually dressed very slowly, stopping often to look at a book or play with Smokey. But this morning she was soon buckling the catches on her overalls and stepping into her shoes.

"Better hurry up, Amy, so we can go," she urged. "Come here, and I'll help you."

Before long breakfast was over, and we were bouncing down the road in the truck, heading for the airstrip and the berry patch. The road was very rocky again because we had had another flood. Hot days causing snow in the high country to melt, plus several days of rain, had made the river rise. We were concerned for a while because our house was so close to the river, but the water did not get any closer than about ten feet from the house. The roads had flooded in several places and caused some inconvenience for many people. The thing that impressed me the most was the noise of rocks bumping along the bottom of the river as the swift current moved them from place to place. That soggy rumble was a sound I'd never heard before.

Sally had liked the water coming into the woods and running along the road. She told us that if she were a river, she would get tired of always going the same way to the lake. She said she would probably like to find new ways like the river did. Then she decided that after a while, she would get tired of exploring and go back to where she belonged. Then the people could use the road again, but they would have to fix it first because she would take some of it with her to remember the fun time.

As we rode along the bumpy path, I said to Sally, "I think the river took too many reminders with it this time."

She wasn't interested in my comment. Both girls were sticking their heads out the window to get a better view of everything.

Sally pulled her head in and said to me, "I like the way some places in the woods are bright with the sun and other places are cool and a little dark from the big trees."

I smiled at her sensitivity and her ability to express it.

"Flowers!" Amy shouted out the window and pointed.

The air from the moving truck must have made the flowers sway because Amy began wagging her head back and forth. Then she saw that we were coming to a creek. "Hello, water," she shouted. She always said hello to the creeks. She seemed satisfied that their bubbling noise was a return greeting.

Sally was back at the window. "Stop at the beaver dam, Mama. I want to see the beaver again."

I stopped the truck near the beaver dam on Battalion Creek. There was a very persistent beaver living there. He continued to dam the creek, which made it cover the road. The men would remedy the problem, and the beaver would rebuild in the same place. We waited quietly for "Mr. Beaver" to come out, but we didn't see him.

"Maybe we'll see him when we come by here on the way home," I said to the disappointed girls.

We wound on down the road, passed the powerhouse, and crossed Company Creek. "Hello, water," Amy shouted again.

The next little road was the one to the airstrip. I drove up it a short distance and parked. We walked the rest of the way. Sally and Amy carried little pails, and I carried a three-pound Crisco can with a handle. Already the sun was warm here in the open. We looked to be sure no plane was wanting to land, even though they seldom did, and then we walked across the rocky strip. Amy stopped periodically to pick up rocks and put them into her pail. She loved rocks and always carried some in her pockets. She seemed to enjoy the way the rocks banged in the empty pail because she kept dropping them in and dumping them out again.

Then we saw them! Berries were all over the side of the airstrip. Sally raced to them and began picking them and dropping them into her pail. She counted as she picked, but when she got to thirty-nine, she started over again. That was as far as she could count.

"Be sure to pick only the black ones," I reminded them. "The red ones and the white ones are not ready to eat yet."

Amy watched Sally take the berries from the stems and put them in the pail. Then Amy dumped her rocks and began picking berries, too. She picked every berry she saw, regardless of color. We worked quietly for a few minutes, enjoying the work and the warmth of the sun. Then I turned and saw that Amy had wandered a good ways from us. I called her back, and soon the pattern was repeated again. The berries farther down always looked better to her. The minute she discovered how the berries tasted, she began eating them and putting very few in the pail. By the time we headed for home, her hands and face were purple. She had discovered that the best part of berrypicking is eating the berries right off the vines. We did manage to take enough berries home to make a pie for Daddy for dinner and one batch of jam.

As we went on these delightful expeditions together, I began to understand how I could answer my professor's maddening statement to me. I had enrolled in a short story correspondence course through the University of Washington in Seattle. My first assignment had been to write about myself. I had written about our coming to Stehekin. The professor had commented on the margin of my paper that we were no doubt escaping from the world. I resented his comment but didn't know how to respond to it yet. I wanted to tell him he was wrong, but I needed some proof. I looked back over all the adjustments we'd had to make and forward at the unknown adjustments ahead. I'd always thought escaping was a final sort of thing. One escaped and lived happily ever after in uninterrupted bliss. That certainly had not been our experience. As the need for adjustment slackened and I began to be able to take the valley as it was, accepting it on its own terms, I began to see that we indeed had not escaped. We were not running away from the world; rather, we were moving into it in a new way and at new levels. Who could guess what that might mean for us?

5

One day at the end of July Tom came home with bad news.

"We have to move to another house," he announced.

"Move?" I was shocked. "Why?"

"The powers in charge have decided that too many repairs are needed on this house before winter, and besides the water is not the quality the county health department thinks it should be. We know a new septic tank is needed," Tom explained. (Tom's dad had nearly fallen into the septic tank while cutting weeds in the backyard.)

I dropped into a chair. "Move?" I wailed again. "But we just moved here!" I looked around the living room. "We just got everything unpacked."

Tom sat down with weariness. "I know. All that work! And it's just beginning to seem like home."

"Where do they want us to move to?" I was almost afraid to ask.

"Down the road to the old Russell cabin. You know, that one in the open area near the bridge." He sat up, and his face brightened. "It's really not a bad house."

"When do we have to move?"

"Not for a while. They have to do some carpentry work inside. There are no closets or cabinets."

I groaned. I could just imagine what it would be like if it didn't even have closets or cabinets.

We went to look at the house. It was smaller than the one we were in, but despite my not wanting to, we couldn't help falling in love with it. It had vertical cedar siding outside. The living room and the kitchen area were in the front of the house, and the two bedrooms and bath were behind them. The living room had two four-by-eight windows and the kitchen a four-by-six window. The walls were paneled in all rooms. A large storage room with shelves was connected to the house and accessible through a covered porch area. Our main disappointment was that we would have to give up our huge fireplace. This house had a stone-covered area in which a Franklin stove would be placed.

Tom saw my disappointment. "Well anyway, a Franklin will heat the house better. We won't lose so much heat with it."

At the time it seemed a small consolation, but we later found this to be an asset, for it did in fact keep the house warmer. We had to admit we had been cold in the other house, even on rainy summer evenings.

The location was wonderful. It was in an open area with a beautiful meadow in front of it. Numerous huge mountain maple trees dotted the meadow. There was an awesome view of mountains across the meadow. Woods crept into the backyard, and a small stream, an offshoot of the river, meandered by. The thought of another move still depressed me, but I could see this house was in much better shape. The view out the huge front windows won my heart.

"There's so much open space for the girls to play," Tom noted.

"Yes, and best of all, I won't have to worry about Amy being so near the river."

Tom was especially happy that this house was two miles closer to the school. That proved to be a blessing in the winter.

With the realization that we would have to move again tucked in the back of our minds, we began to get ready for the coming school year. The schoolhouse was made of logs. There was electricity but no water. There were two outhouses in back, one for girls and one for boys. The main room of the school was about eighteen by twenty-five feet. Two additions had been made: a small back room to house a teacher and a shelter to cover the wood supply. The inside walls of the school were of a material that resembled bulletin boards. It had been painted bright yellow with orange trim. The floor was Masonite. The benches and cabinets were dirty and filled with mouse nests. The books were also dirty, and most were of a 1940 vintage. The desks were marred and still contained goodies from last spring's lunches. It was hard to decide where to begin.

The first day we worked some of the valley people came to help. We appreciated it. But still Tom and I spent six full days discarding, cleaning, scrubbing, mopping, and moving bookcases and the metal cabinet. Tom's cousin, Edith, came to visit us from Ohio and helped us get the schoolhouse ready. Her main job was to clean the desks. She also looked after the girls while Tom and I worked. We did everything we could think of to improve the school. Finally we realized the only thing that would really help was a paint job. By secret means we obtained two gallons of celery green wall paint and one gallon of white enamel. What a fantastic difference the new paint made! The valley people seemed as surprised as we were.

Word got out that we were changing the school, and all kinds of people "wandered by" and decided to stop in. We greeted them, exchanged a few words, and kept right on working. I think everyone in the valley saw my blue-jeaned behind sticking out of a storage cabinet or my red bandana bobbing as I painted doorjambs. Most people didn't say much to us, but the rumor was the schoolhouse was cleaner than it had been the day it was built. Two nights before school began, we had the place ready. The desks were in the traditional rows, with the little ones on one side and the bigger ones on the other. Bulletin boards decorated the walls and enticed the children to the reading corner. We were very pleased.

When we went to school on Labor Day to put up the new American flag, we saw the front porch was dusty from all the people who had come to look in the shiny-clean windows. By golly it really looked like a schoolhouse!

We were a little nervous the first day of school. We'd been told by various people that we might have discipline problems, so we came on strong from the beginning. All seven of the kids had come to school for a couple of hours before the first day of school to be tested by Tom. So before school began, we had some idea where to start each child.

The children arrived with one or both of their parents. The children were scrubbed clean, and many of them had on new clothes. They looked a bit uncomfortable and as though they really would rather have been running and playing in the woods or even doing chores at home. We quickly realized they were as uneasy as we were.

We started with pledging our allegiance to the flag. The voices were very quiet. Either they weren't speaking up, or they didn't know the pledge. We found later that both were true. Tom put the flag in the holder outside. Not a child moved while he was out of the room. I sat at the back of the room. Maybe the kids felt they had been ganged up on. There were two of us and only seven of them. Sally's eyes were big and round, taking everything in.

Tom proceeded to present the rules to the kids. He read them from his clipboard, sounding like a tough head coach. They seemed a little amazed that he was giving all these rules, but he announced them in such a manner that the children weren't ready, at this time anyway, to dispute him. They even co-operated when he showed them explicitly how they were to wash their hands. They were to line up. The first child was to pour water in the basin, wash hands with soap, rinse in the water, and then dump the water. Then the same child was to pour water in the basin for the next child. The bigger children were to help pour for the little ones. Tom explained that he expected the classroom to stay clean, including the books. (He had gotten some new ones from his former students at the private school where he had taught, and we had bought a set of readers for the young children.) The main way to keep things clean was to keep our hands clean.

Tom called each child up to his desk and gave him or her a set of books. The chalkboard listed all the assignments for that day. If a student had questions and the teacher was busy, then he should go on to something he could do alone until the teacher could come to help him. Tom told them he expected to be called

Mr. Olson, and I would be called Mrs. Olson. The kids had been accustomed to calling their teachers by their first names.

Everyone began to work on their lessons, and I took the two second graders into the back room to begin their reading lesson. Tom began working individually with the others. Later I worked with Sally on reading. She was the only first grader, so she and I worked alone. She seemed excited and eager to learn from us.

At recess everyone went outside. It was good to get rid of some of the stiffness from the room. The younger children began to run and chase. A basketball hoop was nailed to a tree, and the three older boys began to toss the ball at the basket. Few were going into the hoop. Tom watched awhile and then offered to show them how to improve on their skill. He threw the ball five times and made a basket every single time. He told me later he couldn't believe it. The kids were duly impressed, and esteem for Mr. Olson went up another notch.

At lunchtime everyone ran out to eat at the picnic table under the tree. I went home to be with Amy and Edith.

Edith asked, "How's it going?"

"Very well," I sighed. "Unbelievably well. Tom's being rough on them, but maybe if he starts out really strict, they will get in line and then he can let up later."

After school I picked them up. "Well, what do you think?" I asked.

"Great so far," he sighed. "I'm tired."

"What do you think, Sally?"

"It's fun," she said. "Mr. Olson is a good teacher."

Tom smiled and gave her a one-armed hug. "Miss Olson is a good student, too."

After school started, our lives began to settle into a routine. I helped Tom at school with the youngest children for a couple of hours in the morning. Amy went along and played quietly (most of the time) or made pictures or looked at books. Sometimes she sat on my lap, listening while I taught. It's no wonder she could read before she was four.

The afternoons were my quiet time while Amy napped. When school was out, we all hurried into the woods to cut more wood.

In the evening I usually found myself alone by the fire because Tom was exhausted from teaching all day and cutting and stacking wood. I enjoyed the quiet by the fire. I read or reflected on the day's happenings. Sometimes I tried to write down my thoughts and feelings. Often the writing would end up as a letter to my parents. One evening in the midst of the woodcutting time I wrote this letter to my parents:

"Do you have any idea what goes into gathering eleven cords of wood? We didn't until September 18th when we started. Let me tell you, if anyone wants to lose weight, tell them to fell eighteen trees, cut off the branches, cut the log in spools about twenty-two inches long, split the spools into usable-sized pieces (four to twelve wedges per spool), load them on the truck, unload them, and stack them in the shelter. I guarantee they'll lose weight!

"One of the most awesome things I've ever seen is one of those big trees falling. Tom cuts a big wedge in the base of the standing tree. The wedge faces the place he wants the tree to fall. Then he cuts through the back of the tree so that the cut will come out a little below the center of the wedge. The tree begins to groan and creak and sway. It seems an eternity that we stand there behind it, well out of its way, and wait for it to start falling. My heart races, and my stomach gets butterflies in those long moments. Slowly, slowly, it begins to fall. It hangs in the air for an instant. Tom yells, 'Timber!' The woods are filled with a roar as the magnificent tree picks up momentum. If another tree is near enough, it smacks that tree, ripping off branches or snapping off a dead top. By this time we are trembling silently as we watch the fantastic force we have put into motion. At last the giant, now many times bigger than it seemed when it was standing, crashes into the ground. The deafening thud echoes through the forest as we stand in silent wonder. It is some moments before we move out from our place of watching to view the majestic creature. A look at all the rings makes me wander back in time to the days when this was only a sapling. How long it has taken to become such a monarch. How quickly came its final end. I wonder what made it die. How many creatures must have lived in it, scurried up and down it, flown over it. How many snows were piled at its base. How many men and women could have rushed past during its time, bent on their own worth and their own problems. How many stars it must have seen and sunrises it must have witnessed as it reached upward, groping for the heavens. Well it isn't through yet. It will warm a house for a happy family. It will cook a roast or a pie for a hungry and tired family. Its ashes will return to the soil, nourishing another sapling, nudging it on to become another magnificent monarch."

As the days passed and our lives became more settled, I began to realize that the calling that had brought us to this place was once more making itself known. It became a stirring, an excitement, an anticipation. "We're in the right place. There is a reason for our being here, and we're going to find it."

In this paradise of nature my thoughts began to sense the patterns of creation. I could see and feel the orderliness of things as God had made them. I began to remember that God had made me. Could there be a pattern to my life? Could there be an orderliness in it? It had had a beginning, just as those trees had, and surely it would have an end, too. What would it be? Would there have been meaning to it? I had no answers, just questions. But the stirring inside me assured me there were answers and that I would find them here in this place.

A Christian catalog came in our mail one day. With mild interest I looked through it and saw a plaque for sale. It read, "God's Peace Be in This House." I ordered it without knowing why. When it arrived, I asked Tom to put it up.

He looked puzzled. "You really want that up in the living room?"

I nodded.

"Where?"

"Over the front door."

"Why?"

I looked at him a moment. "I don't know why, but I do."

"Okay," he shrugged. "I guess we can always use a little peace."

That night I took my childhood Bible down from the shelf. I turned through the pages without really reading any words. I was just feeling them, I guess. I saw places marked with pencil and others underlined with ink.

"These words were meaningful for me once," I thought. "Maybe they will be again. Maybe some of the answers are in here."

I sat in front of the fire, holding the closed Bible and feeling the peace that the sign announced. After a while I put another log on the fire and went to bed.

6

Fall arrived. The air was crisp and frosty in the mornings. The noonday sun was only warm. The sunlight cast long shadows. The vine maples and dogwoods became tipped with orange and red. The river lazily frittered along in its narrow bed, only dreaming of the days it rushed and tumbled over the exposed rocks. I fancied that it wondered how it ever bullied huge trees and stones down its path. The bears returned from the high country for their last fling before hibernating. They investigated our garbage cans and ate from our apple tree while they waited for the salmon to begin spawning. The highest mountain peaks began to collect white, fluffy material to fashion their winter caps. The landing was sparsely populated. Boat docks were empty. Summer cottages were once more dozing behind their boarded windows. The woods echoed with the whine of chain saws and the ring of axes as the men gathered their winter's supply of wood. They were prodded by the chilly evenings that hinted of long, cold nights ahead.

The schoolhouse was bustling. A pleasant curl of smoke rose from the chimney. The American flag swayed proudly from a log column on the front porch. A picnic table waited patiently under the tall pines for the children to bring their lunch bags. An ax rested in the chopping block next to the woodshed. Outside all was quiet except for the subdued rushing of Rainbow Falls. Inside Beethoven's Fifth Symphony poured out of the record player, or quiet voices conferred over the open books. The youngest children earnestly announced the messages in their new reading books. A bucket of water fetched from Rainbow Creek stood next to the enamel washbowl on the counter. A large tin can sat in the corner. It was filled with provisions to feed the children should they become snowbound at school.

As snow clouds gathered and the temperature dropped, Tom and I began to panic. We had not moved to the new house yet. Would we have to do it in the snow? Finally, the week before Thanksgiving, we were given the go-ahead. It was a frantic move. We made what seemed like five thousand trips up and down the road, shuffling improperly packed boxes. Valley people helped us with the heavy items. Just as we made the last trip, snow began to fall. I didn't mind the disarray inside so much when I saw the white stuff piling up outside. Even if I couldn't find a thing I needed, at least it was all in the house someplace, and it got there without fighting a snowstorm.

We also had our winter's supply of wood gathered. We had all four worked at it. Tom felled the trees and split them into sizes Sally and I could handle. We carried it to the truck while Amy gathered small pieces for the kindling box. When the truck was filled, we drove home. Sally and I unloaded while Tom stacked. It was a great day when the woodshed was full.

Everyone in the valley was engaged in the same activity. "Do you have your wood in?" was the main topic of conversation whenever people gathered to get mail or pick up children or just to visit. Occasionally the power went off during the early fall. We would all laugh and say, "Who did it? Who hit a power line when they felled a tree?" Even though everyone laughed, we also cringed for fear that sometime we would display our lack of woodsmen's expertise and hit a line. Then everyone in the valley would know we couldn't make the tree fall where we wanted it to.

Sally's sixth birthday arrived. We had a small party with the family and the other little girl in the valley. We played games, sang "Happy Birthday," and ate cake and ice cream. It was like any other birthday party except it was very small. Sally was happy. She said that even God gave her a present because it snowed that day. It's amazing that children often recognize the source of their gifts long before their parents understand.

After we moved to the new house and were settled, I once again became aware of the movings in my heart. It was impossible not to be aware of it because everything I saw was beautiful and intricately made and provided for. Everything I did and everywhere I turned, I was surrounded by God's works.

One morning after the first snows had come and gone, I was hanging laundry on the clothesline. The cold nipped at my fingers, and steam rose off the clothes. As I put my hands in my pockets to warm them, I heard a barking sound. I wondered where it came from because there were no dogs around. I had heard coyotes many times in the night but never in the morning, and this didn't sound like the barking that sometimes preceded the howling of the coyotes. Then I realized the sound was coming from above me. I looked up to see a large flock of geese struggling to get into formation. One bird after another burst into the lead as the others tried, amid a great noise of honking, to form behind it. Eventually one bird won the leadership, and the other geese obediently flapped into place. With a more harmonious chorus of honks they disappeared from my view. "There it is again," I thought. "God has an order and pattern for everything in His creation. And isn't it beautiful! But what does that mean for me?"

I loved being outdoors. There was something warm and special glowing in me whenever I was outside. Everything from the colored leaves to the sight of last summer's fawns peering at me through the tall grass seemed to feed the fire within me. I felt as though I were a David Livingstone or a Meriwether Lewis discovering new creations as I explored new territory. Tom and I and the girls spent a great deal of time walking through the meadows and woods. The sights and sounds and smells seemed to intoxicate us. At first we stayed on established trails, and later we struck out on our own. I remember one walk in particular.

It was a Sunday late in November. Amy was taking her nap, so I laced up my hiking boots, pulled on my jacket, and said goodbye to Tom, who was splitting wood for kindling, and Sally, who was playing house under the sagging branches of a large mountain maple tree. I walked across the meadow toward the mountains. The previous snowfalls had melted except in small patches in the shadow of the trees. The air was chilly on my face, and I pulled my hood over my head. I jammed my hands into my pockets and looked overhead. Gray, fat snow clouds were sitting on the mountains. It wouldn't be long before we had another snowfall. I quickened my pace and headed toward the woods. As I crossed the end of the meadow, I walked along a small stream. In the middle of the widest part of the stream was a beaver lodge. I slowed my pace, hoping to catch a glimpse of the beavers living there. I stopped and stood very still, and presently a little brown head popped up in the water. The beaver paddled to the edge of the pond and, taking some branches in its mouth, headed back to the lodge. As I watched, it disappeared around the side of the lodge.

I walked on into the woods, and my arrival was noted by a Steller's jay. His large plume on the top of his head bobbed and flicked as he hopped on the branch and scolded me. Steller's jays are beautiful birds, with their bright blue bodies and black heads and plumes. But these jays have the most irritable dispositions of any bird around. One came to our bird feeder beside the cabin, and it would not allow any other bird to eat at the feeder. Even when it wasn't eating, it sat high in a tree and swooped down on any bird that attempted to eat there. I wondered if God had really intended for such a beautiful creature to be so obnoxious.

I walked on into the woods and left the irritated bird behind. I climbed a small hill and entered the heart of the woods. As I walked, I began to breathe deeply the crisp air filled with the aroma of wood, dried leaves, and damp earth. As I went downhill, I began to smell fish. At the bottom of the hill I found a stream literally filled with salmon. They had made their way here to spawn. Some were busy attending to the last work of their lives. Others had finished their work and were floating limply, content to let the waves from the other fish push them here and there as they waited to die. For some time I sat beside the stream and watched.

"What a spectacle!" I thought. "How sad, and yet how lovely. These fish had a reason for living, and they knew what that reason was. They were born in this stream and found their way out into the lake, where they lived and grew. When the right time came, they found their way back here and completed their life cycle.

How do they know where to come? There are many streams feeding the lake. How do they know which one is the one they were hatched in?"

As I watched, the smell of the woods enveloped me. The air became filled with a living stillness. I was sitting quietly, but my heart was racing. Then I knew.

"God is here. He made all this. This stream and these fish, this woods and these mountains, they are His because He made them. But He didn't just make them and leave them. *He is here.* God is here; I am here, too." I looked around. Maybe I expected to see God, but nothing happened. I sat there for some time, absorbing the knowledge that God was here and that I was here.

At last I got up and headed toward home. The strong feeling I'd had began to fade, and yet the knowing stayed. God was here, and I knew it not just in my head. Now I knew it in my heart.

Then the question came: "If God is here and I am here, what does that mean for me? God is in His creations. Aren't I one of His creations? Is it possible that what I've read in the Bible and learned in Sunday School as a child is really true? I mean actually so, not just a pretty way of saying things? Could this really mean that God is in me?"

I was deep in thought as I left the woods and started through the meadow. Something cold splashing on my face brought me back to the present. Snow was falling in big flakes. Already it was beginning to cover the ground. I walked quickly across the meadow toward home. Outside I was cold, but inside a new warmth glowed.

With renewed interest I began to read my Bible every spare moment. I knew the answer was there, and I devoured it with a voracious appetite. I read one Gospel after another. Tom must have wondered what was happening to me. I never spoke to him about it because I didn't really know what to say, but I often looked up from reading my Bible to see him watching me. Then one morning, after another snowstorm, the answer came.

I was standing at the front window, looking out over the meadow at the new-fallen snow piled on the old snow. The weather was cold enough now so that the snows did not melt between storms. I saw fresh snow stacked on the tree branches, bending them down. Snow lay on all the crags of the mountains. The world had, in fact, turned white.

As I looked, the sun broke through the clouds, and it was so bright on the snow I had to squint my eyes. But the sun was not shining indiscriminately. It was shining directly on an object at the edge of the meadow. I had never seen that object before. But there it stood in the sunlight. And there was no snow on it. It was a cross.

I did not ask myself how it got there or why it didn't have snow on it. I just stared as it seared its way into my mind and heart. Tears rolled down my cheeks. The bonds around my heart and mind broke, and I had the answer. God is not just the God of Creation. He is *my* God. And because of His Son Jesus and the cross on which He died, I am His.

7

Winter hit hard. For ten days the temperature hovered between ten and minus ten. That caused many problems because our usual temperatures were not that cold. We lost our water supply. Our water came by gravity flow down a mountain and through a large wooden pipe from a small reservoir on Company Creek. The power for the valley was generated by the rushing waters of the same creek. As the temperature dropped lower and lower, the creek began to freeze.

Two or three times a day Tom would go up the hill behind the powerhouse to the reservoir. He pounded the forming ice and broke it into pieces so the water would flow into the pipe. It was cold, hard work. Sometimes the girls and I would bundle up, take the sled, and go with him. He looked like an ice fisherman hacking away at the ice. When he had done all he could, we would pull the girls back down the hill on the sled. At home the fire was deliciously warm, and the steaming cocoa burned our mouths. How good it was to be home!

Finally there was such a small amount of water going through the powerhouse that the whole valley was without power. As a result our little reservoir was tapped. After a couple of days of very erratic power, things stabilized, and our reservoir wasn't needed. But by then the water level was so low that the reservoir had frozen. We were without water for five weeks! Tom got very good at scrambling down snowy banks with a three-gallon bucket and dipping water out of the icy creek, and eventually we worked out a system for cooking and washing dishes, bathing, and washing clothes.

I found myself conserving every drop of water. If the same drop could be used more than once before it went down the drain, it was! One evening I was dipping water out of one of the buckets that stood in the middle of the kitchen floor. I stopped as my mind flashed back to last summer—was it only last summer?—when I had been so aghast at seeing Mitch's friends dipping into water buckets. Now I was having to do it. A new understanding! "Lord, it looks like I'm growing."

The hardest part about being without water for city dudes like us was using an outhouse in zero-degree weather. One evening Sally returned to the cabin after a trip to the outhouse. As she blew out the candle in the lantern and set it down, she stomped the snow off her boots. Unzipping her jacket, she said, "I think I'll wait till spring to go to the bathroom again."

I agreed with her. It was a nuisance to have to bundle up, light the lantern, and take a freezing walk. And sitting down on an ice cube is never pleasant unless you're a polar bear. But an unexpected benefit emerged from the whole episode. Before my nightly treks I'd never realized how lovely the dark, clear nights were. Unless there was some kind of moon, the night was tangibly black. I remember the darkness as one of my first experiences after moving to the wilderness. It was so dark I could see absolutely nothing. I moved my hand toward my face, wondering when I would be able to see it. I hit my nose before I saw my hand. The first weeks we lived there, I would wake up at night and think I'd gone blind. There was nothing but darkness so real it seemed I could touch it. I immediately ordered, by mail, an alarm clock that had an illuminated dial. When I saw it, I knew I had not gone blind.

The outhouse trips confirmed the tangible darkness. The world was totally black and white: white where the candlelight reflected the snow on either side of the trench we had dug to the outhouse, black beyond the reach of the light. All at once I really understood what Jesus had meant when he said, "I am the light of the world: he that followeth me shall not walk in darkness, but shall have the light of life" (John 8:12).

As the tiny new life in my heart and mind grew, it constantly cried to be fed. Every spare moment I feasted from the pantry of the Scriptures. I was amazed at the beauty and relevance of these ancient writings. They clearly spoke about my own life. These words graphically described me and where I had been; I believed they also knew where I could go and what I could be if I chose to do so. It seemed that I began to live in the Scriptures as they began to live in me.

I loved to stand outside on clear nights and gaze at the stars. They were much brighter here than anywhere else I'd seen them, and there were many more visible. As I stood there alone in the dark, it seemed I could hear God speaking to Abraham, "Look toward heaven, and number the stars, if you are able to number them. . . . So shall your descendants be. And he believed the Lord; and he reckoned it to him as righteousness" (Gen. 15:5-6 RSV).

As I stood in the winter night, looking at the moon and stars, I marveled with the psalmist: "When I consider thy heavens, the work of thy fingers, the moon and the stars, which thou hast ordained; What is man, that thou art mindful of him? and the son of man, that thou visitest him?" (Ps. 8:3-4).

It was a miracle to me that the God who made all this knew and loved me. But because of the cross in the sunlight that winter day, I knew that I was loved above these inanimate creations. And what that knowledge did in my heart! I could really sing the last verse of that psalm: "O Lord our Lord, how excellent is thy name in all the earth!" (Ps. 8:9).

Still I did not talk with Tom about my new understanding. We had talked a lot in college about God. Tom had felt that God was a good heavenly being who created the world and its systems and then let it go. He felt that God was interested enough in His creation to watch it but that He would not interfere with it. Tom's God was not involved with His world or His people.

I was coming to understand that God was and is involved in His world daily, even to the point of sending His Son to redeem *me*, but I could not share this with Tom. It was almost as though I was pregnant. Something beautiful and vital was growing inside of me, but I could not share it until its time was completed and it was born.

The Lord taught me something else in the night. One night after the girls were tucked into bed, Tom and I started out on our nightly trip to the creek for the morning's water. This particular night there was a full moon. Because it had been cold so long, a heavy crust had formed on the snow, and it easily supported our weight. It was a pleasant quarter-mile walk to the creek. The sled and buckets slipped along easily behind us. We filled the buckets at the creek and left its mischievous giggling and splashing. We started back, walking hand in hand, absorbing the world around us. We were completely alone in our world. No other human was within a mile. We walked slowly in an effort to make the night last longer.

I was enchanted. It seemed to me that we were walking on a field of diamonds. Each snowflake reflected the light of the moon, and what a beautiful world they made because of it. "Isn't it amazing how each one of these snowflakes reflects the light of the moon?" I whispered to Tom.

"Um hum. It is beautiful." His voice was hushed.

"It makes the night much brighter and much more lovely. Why don't we do that?"

"What do you mean?"

I looked up at him. I had always thought he was very handsome, but tonight he seemed even more so. Contentment and strength were in his face. The tuft of dark, curly hair that had pushed its way from under the stocking cap and fallen over his forehead gave him a boyish look.

"Do you believe that each one of these snowflakes is different?" I asked him.

"That's what they say," he replied, smiling.

"And yet each one of them is reflecting the light of the moon," I pursued my thought.

"And—"

"We should be reflecting the light of the Son. Think how the world would be if each of us unique individuals reflected the light of the Son."

"The sun?"

"Yes the S-o-n."

"Oh!" he said thoughtfully.

We were quiet the rest of the way home, but words raced through my head. "I *must* reflect the light of the Son. Oh I *want* to reflect the light of the Son."

Before going into the cabin, I turned back to look at the enchanted night.

"How do I do it?" I asked. There was no answer in the night, but I knew where I could find the answer. As soon as the last chore was done, I sat in front of the fire with my Bible in my hands. How I loved reading it. It was God's own word to me. It was truly a living word because each time I read it, I received more life.

Soon it became evident that no water would ever come down our pipe till spring thawed it. We were not anxious to carry water all winter if it could be helped. After we went to Seattle for Christmas to be with Tom's sister's family, we found that Karl's father had come to our rescue in our absence. He had worked out a crazy system consisting of an old pump and well up the road and garden hoses. The last hose came in our bathroom window and hooked into our water system at the washing machine. The secret of its success was to keep the water flowing all the time; otherwise it would freeze up in the hose. We didn't want to keep filling up the septic tank either, so at night Tom doubled over the hose near where it screwed into our pipes and disconnected it. I opened the bathroom window, and he tossed the hose out. It seemed very simple except that in the morning he had to go outside and get the hose. I held it while he came back in to squeeze it off and connect it. Sometimes the hose froze even though water was running through it. Then we'd have to drag the whole thing into the house and thaw it out. After we had a good amount of snowfall, things got better for us. The snow insulated the hose, and it didn't freeze. Also the hose would never get out of reach of the bathroom window because of the high snowbank against the side of the house. It was a nuisance, but we learned to live with it by laughing at it. I teased Tom, "City husbands put the cat out at night. You put the water out instead."

Tom was growing, too. Throughout this whole water ordeal I seldom heard him complain. He *had* been a complainer before we came to Stehekin.

I sometimes wondered when I watched him gazing into the fire or looking at the cold sunrise, "Could Tom be changing, too? He isn't reading the Bible, but maybe something is happening inside him, too."

We never discussed this, but we grew in our sharing in other ways. A stronger, richer love became evident between us as we stretched and grew in our demanding environment. We sometimes found we did not need to talk. It was enough just to be together, sitting by the fire in each other's arms.

8

I woke suddenly in the black night. What was that strange sound? I had awakened many nights to hear the roar of snow sliding off the roof. But that was not what I was hearing now. I pulled my robe around me and stuffed my feet into my slippers and crept into the living room. Even in the darkness I saw it. It was raining, and the snow was melting! There was more open space to look out of the window. I rushed to the door and opened it. A warm though wet breeze met me.

"Hurrah!" I shouted. "Spring is here!" I closed the door and ran to wake Tom.

"Guess what? Spring is here! A chinook is blowing, and there's a warm rain!"

I was ecstatic, but somehow Tom could not catch my enthusiasm.

"Good," he mumbled. "That's good. What time is it? Good grief, what are you doing up at this time of night?"

"I was watching it rain and listening to the snow melt," I said as I crawled back under the quilt and snuggled beside him.

"Your feet feel like you were walking in the snow."

By morning we were all excited to see the change. As the days passed, everything changed. New landmarks began to appear out of the snow. The tips of tiny trees poked their way into the open. Smoothly rounded shapes began to be transformed into rocks. A greenish cast spread over the deciduous trees. The air was filled with new gurglings as little streams began to run again. Then it happened. We actually saw the ground! And right at the edge of the retreating snow, flowers appeared. It was as though they were made by magic. One minute a spot was covered with snow, and the next minute a lovely glacier lily was standing there.

Great flocks of robins appeared in the meadow. They hopped, listened, and pulled what Amy thought were rubber bands from the earth.

The days were longer, too. I liked that. In the middle of the winter it had been dark by four-thirty in the afternoon. That made the night very long, and without television or radio we had had to learn to entertain ourselves. We did it with family projects, playing games, and reading. We had read through many books together by the time spring arrived.

As soon as the snow was cleared off the Lake Shore Trail, we went for a hike. Little creeks were filling and rushing into the lake. How delicious the water was and so cold that it made our teeth throb.

People were more talkative everywhere. The conversations at the coffee shop and post office turned to gardens and when did we think we could start planting. People began visiting neighbors that they had seen little of except at the landing on the three mail days each week or the few winter gatherings at the community hall.

"Why don't you come over and see us?" Babe, a friend, asked us.

"We'd like to, Babe, but I don't think we can get up the road on your side of the river," Tom replied.

It was true that the dirt road had turned into a plowed mud path.

"Well I make it every day, so I don't see why you can't."

"Okay, we'll try it tonight. Sally is going to stay all night with Rebecca, so the rest of us will come."

A family with a girl Sally's age had moved to the valley in January. Sally was ecstatic to have a girl friend her age. Rebecca and her family had lived in Alaska under conditions much more severe than ours, so she was a good companion for Sally. Tom and I enjoyed her parents; and Amy, her little sister, Monya.

After dinner that evening we started up the valley in our truck. For a while it seemed to be fine.

"This isn't so bad," Tom said.

Around the next curve we ground our way through a mud patch. Then we hit it.

"I guess I spoke too soon," Tom admitted, and we involuntarily slowed to a crawl.

Then we stopped moving, even though the wheels were still going around. Tom removed his foot from the accelerator and opened the door.

"Oh no!"

I opened my door and gasped. The mud was nearly up to the door of the truck!

"Cripes!" Tom shouted. "I knew we shouldn't have tried it tonight! Now look at the mess we're in! There's no way we can get out by ourselves. How in the world did Babe ever get through this? Stay here. I'm going to walk across the field and back to his house."

Amy and I waited. Soon we saw the light of a snowmobile coming across the field. It came as close to the road as the presence of snow allowed. Babe and Tom walked to the side of the road. Babe shook his head and laughed. "You really did it this time, Olson."

Tom was angry. "You said you could get through it. I shouldn't have listened to you."

"I was getting through it, but this evening I almost didn't make it. It's worse than it was this morning. Come on. I'll take Lois and Amy back to the house and get my pickup."

"What can you do with your truck? There's no way you can pull me out of this."

"Maybe I can push you out."

"Push me out? That's the craziest thing I've ever heard. You'll bog down just like I am and worse because you'll be trying to push."

"Well then I'll be stuck with you. Come on, Lois."

Tom stepped into the mud, and I handed Amy across to him. Then I stepped out of the truck. Instantly I felt a force pulling at my boots. When I tried to pull my foot up, the mud struggled to take the boot right off my foot. "Are you sure this isn't quicksand?" I shouted to them as I tried to walk to the side of the road.

"Might as well be," Tom grumbled as he took my hand and pulled me up onto firmer ground.

He waited while Amy and I rode with Babe on the snowmobile back to his house. His wife, Bernita, was waiting cheerfully and seemed glad to see us despite the mess we were in. Babe left with his pickup, and it was some time before he and Tom came walking back.

"I can't believe it," Tom said as they came into the house after leaving their boots on the porch. "He just plowed right into that mud and nosed up to our truck. It never moved an inch. There they sit. Right in the middle of the road. Radiator to radiator."

Babe was chortling as he handed Tom a cup of coffee. "Nobody's going down that road tonight. Anyway if they did, they'd have to push us out before they could get past. Sit down. Might as well plan to stay the night with us."

"Well we're here. We may as well enjoy ourselves."

We did. In the morning Babe and Tom walked to the road and found the trucks waiting patiently in the mudhole. While we were eating Bernita's delicious sourdough pancakes, Babe contacted Wally over the CB-type radio. Wally came to our rescue.

"Olson, what did you do this time?" his voice growled over the radio. "Miles, you're as crazy as he is. What were you guys doing anyway?"

"Morning, Wally. How about getting the grader and pulling us out?" Babe answered.

"I reckon if anyone is ever to use this road again, I'll have to," he replied, with many other stronger words sprinkled through the statement.

By noon we were on our way home again, laughing and saying that it really was stupid, but it was a lot of fun, too.

Our housecleaning and school-cleaning job changed from cleaning up wet, melting snow spots to cleaning up brown, oozy globs. We still wore our rubberized winter boots, not for warmth, but for protection in the mud. The schoolchildren began to play in a tiny stream of water that found its way down the mountain behind the school. They accomplished all kinds of damming projects and earned some antagonism from the teacher-janitor who had to contend with rerouted water flows as well as soggy students.

Late in the spring gardens were plowed, and the end of May saw tiny plants that had been started inside months before being set out. The trees had leafed out, birds sang and darted everywhere, and I could once again hang laundry outside to dry. Mountain bluebells, lupine, Indian paintbrush, tiger lilies, and other gorgeous flowers decorated the countryside. It was a glorious time to be alive. I had not been lonely that winter. There was no time for it. Everything was so new and required my whole attention. But now that it was spring and I could be outdoors again for longer periods and with little effort, I realized that I was really glad winter was over. I felt very proud, too. It had not been a particularly hard winter, weatherwise, but we had survived. We'd made it. And that was worth something.

"Thank You, Lord," I said. "We've grown a lot, haven't we? We've grown within, together, and toward You. It's been a good winter."

After the mud problem resolved itself, we made a big decision. We bought a car. We had discovered that being at the other end of the lake without a car was a problem. It was difficult to do the errands, get groceries, and do anything else without a car. We seldom went downlake, but when we did, we needed a car. It had been very difficult to get to Seattle last Christmas, too. We decided to send our truck downlake on the barge and buy an old Stehekin car we'd found sitting under a tree. It was a '56 Ford ranch wagon and had spent all its life on the Stehekin roads. It looked it. It had been deposited under a tree by its owner when it became more trouble than it was worth. It had good tires and two sets of chains. We bought it from Harry Buckner, one of the first Stehekin homesteaders, for forty dollars. With minor encouragement it started right up, and we drove it directly to the shop for an overhaul and tune-up. It turned out to be quite a venture and a substantial investment. But we did not often regret it. Besides it made us seem more like real Stehekin folks.

Summer tumbled in quickly on the heels of spring. We fished the lake for salmon and trout and built a smoker to preserve the fish. Our cabin was constantly filled with guests, as family and friends came "to see what we had gotten ourselves into." Tom and I also directed the first of four summer backpacking camps. They were times of great growth for us and, we hoped, for the young people who came with us.

In no time, it seemed, I was putting away the shorts and getting out the warm jackets. The valley was quiet again, and I felt a closeness to it as my life, too, began to quiet down after the summer of camping and hosting and gardening. Tom and I were glad to spend long evenings together by the fire once more with steaming mugs of cocoa, music, and books. Once more I allowed the hunger for more Scripture to be a part of my life.

One night late in November I laid aside my Bible and announced I was going to take a walk. It was cold outside, but not much snow had fallen yet. I pulled on my boots, zipped up my parka, tied my hood, and waved a mittened hand to Tom as I disappeared into the night. I did not take a lantern or flashlight. I was going to depend on the half-moon for light.

I chuckled to remember my first hikes and how I'd been afraid, even in broad daylight. Here I was, roaming the woods at night. I walked down our road a quarter mile to the bridge across the river. I stood on the bridge for a while, watching the constant rushing and tumbling of the water. Then I walked down to the river's edge and stood among the trees, hoping to see an animal come to drink. I was not disappointed. A coyote very cautiously crept to the river. I loved to see the coyotes, and I saw them often. I had seen coyotes in the tall grass of the meadow and had walked to within ten feet of one before it turned and ran. Tom and I had witnessed one trotting back and forth across the meadow as it carried its kill home in pieces to the pups. One night I had been startled by a coyote standing about two feet from our front window, looking in at me. But this coyote at the river was not so bold. It caught my scent and left after one quick drink.

As I wandered from the river into the woods, I began to sense that I was not alone. I was being followed. I turned and looked behind me but saw nothing. I walked a little faster, but the presence stayed with me. I began to question the wisdom of coming out into the woods at night. I was no longer afraid of the woods or the animals, and as far as I knew, there were no other people around. And yet there definitely was something with me. I turned toward the meadow and home. As I came into the clearing of the meadow, I stopped. The mountains formed a rim around my horizon. The sky was flecked with stars like a piece of black dotted swiss. A cold wind began to blow in my face.

I was no longer following or being followed. I was totally surrounded, and I was not afraid. The presence was Jesus.

"Follow me," He said.

And I followed. We crossed the meadow and stood looking at my cabin. It was nestled in the shadows of the woods. Snow was piled around it. The cold wind blew round it. But there it stood, a beautiful, warm glow radiating from it. I could see a fire burning brightly in the fireplace. Warmth and love and peace and shelter reached out to me in the cold night. I wanted to go in, but Jesus spoke again.

"See that home. See how it glows with warmth and love. Feel how it calls to you in the darkness. Even the wild coyote is drawn by its light. Even the wildest of My creatures wants its warmth and light.

"The night is long and dark for many of My children. They do not know Me. They are alone in the coldness. Be, for Me, a cabin in the night woods. Let Me build a fire on your hearth. Let Me fill you with warmth and light. Let My light shine out in the dark so even My wildest creatures will come to you for warmth. For when you open your door to them, they will come in to Me.

"Be for Me a cabin in the dark woods."

9

"Tom, let's start a Bible study group here."

It was the evening after my walk in the woods. Tom put down the book he was reading.

"What?"

"Let's start a Bible study group."

"That's what I thought you said." He looked at me with a puzzled look in his eyes.

A great desire to share my experience of last night and my new faith and purpose rushed up in me. But as quickly as it sprang up, it was checked.

"Not yet. Not yet," I heard an inner voice say. "He must come on his own. I will tell you when."

I looked at the note in my hand and broke the silence. "Here's a notice we can put on the bulletin board at the post office. Everyone in the valley will be sure to see it there. Maybe someone will be interested."

Tom still stared at me. He took the card from me and read, "'Bible study at the Olsons. Wednesday night. 7:30. Everyone welcome.' Are you sure you want to do this? I mean, that is really taking a stand. You know no one here talks about religion, at least not favorably."

"I know that no one talks to me about it. But I don't talk to them, either. Maybe there are lots of people who are interested or who study the Bible by themselves. Maybe they are just waiting for someone else to start something. You know the Byrds would be interested. Bob used to give little talks on Sundays."

"Well—," Tom hesitated. "I don't know. I'm the school-teacher here. Maybe we shouldn't mix the two. Maybe some of the parents wouldn't like it."

"Maybe and maybe not. And since when, Tom Olson, have you become afraid of parents? You've always done what you thought was right. Just because this is a small community shouldn't change that."

"Yeah you're right," he agreed.

We sat for a while, looking at the fire.

"Why do you want to do this?" he asked quietly.

I listened for the voice to tell me to speak, but it was silent. So I said, "I just want to. The Bible is so neat. There is so much in it. Some of it I can understand. I can see what it means for me. But there's a lot I don't understand. I'd like to talk with other people about it. I feel sure it would be a very enriching time."

"What makes you think that anybody here could tell you anything about the Bible? We don't have a minister here. There isn't even a church. There never has been. It would be like the blind leading the blind."

"Maybe," I said. "But we could share our thoughts and feelings anyway. I'd like that. Sometimes I feel, well, lonely. It's so beautiful here, and I love it. But sometimes I feel lonely for people, people I can talk with about things that really matter. Not just surface things."

"I know," he agreed, squeezing my hand in understanding. "I miss that, too."

We were quiet, sipping cocoa. Tom gripped my hand tightly.

"If you put that notice on the bulletin board, you would really be taking a stand," he said. "You'd be making a commitment. There are some people here who won't appreciate it."

"I know that," I said quietly. Turning away from his penetrating eyes, I stared at the fire.

"And what if no one comes?" he said, voicing one of my fears. I took a big breath. "I'll just have to risk that."

We watched as the tongue of fire licked at the wood and the pulsating light played in the darkened room.

"Okay," he agreed. "Go ahead." His arm pulled me close to

him, and his head leaned on mine. I felt loved and protected regardless of the outcome.

The notice went up the next day, Monday. No one said anything to me about it, and by Wednesday evening, I was wondering if anyone would come. By seven o'clock I had the girls in bed. I went to my room and sat down on the bed in the dark.

"Jesus, this evening is Yours. I don't know if anyone will come. That's up to You. I don't even know what to do if somebody does come. I've never been to a Bible study. So, Lord, it's all Yours. Do whatever You want. Thank You."

By seven forty-five seven people had come. Our living room was more than filled. It was an exciting meeting. We decided to meet once a week and to study Matthew chapter by chapter.

That evening was like a pebble thrown into a pond. The ripples made wider and wider circles until undreamed-of consequences resulted. We grew individually; we grew together as a group. We questioned and searched together. We shared what answers we'd found. We differed and debated viewpoints. Some of us prayed very haltingly, and some of us didn't pray at all in the group. It was a treat when one of the Byrd family came. Their prayers were always lovely and inspiring.

That evening I saw the beginning of a new life for Tom. He had always insisted he could not understand the Bible. My mother had given him a Living Bible for Christmas. Now he began to read it. Many of his statements in the study group were prefaced with, "I don't know anything about the Bible, but does this verse mean so and so?" As he read the Bible and questioned, he began to find understanding and meaning for his own life.

We began to talk about the Bible occasionally. Usually it was the evening before the Bible study. But the discussions were limited to gaining more understanding of what the Scriptures said. We carefully avoided any personal applications.

As I watched and prayed for Tom, he began to grow. Many times that fall and winter I stood in the door and waved good-bye to him as he walked off in the night to go to a Bible study. When it was not at our house, he and I traded weeks, one of us going and one staying home with the children.

Then one night I received a beautiful confirmation. I stood in the door and watched Tom wind his way down our path between the banks of snow. In one hand he held his Bible. The other hand steadied the snowshoes resting on his shoulder. He would need them to get from the road to the house where the Bible study was. At the end of our path Tom turned and waved at me with the Bible. The moonlight streamed down on him as the Lord spoke to me.

"This man, your husband, is very special to Me. He will come to Me, and I will call him into My service. I will use him mightily. He will be a man for Me."

10

It was Christmas season again. We would be spending Christmas week at Tom's sister's again, along with his parents. We were looking forward to the time with them. We didn't have room for everyone during the winter months. They had come to our house in the summer when the children could all sleep outside in tents.

We did not want to cut a Christmas tree for such a short time, but we wanted something to help us get into the feel of the season. A friend in Ohio had told me about chrismon trees (Christmas trees decorated with the numerous symbols of the Christian faith), so I decided to adapt that idea for us. I ordered some felt from a fabric store in Wenatchee, then made a two-foot green felt Christmas tree and hung it on the back of the front door. Each night for seven nights before we left for Seattle we had a family devotion time. We talked about the seven "I am" statements Jesus made. One of the girls made a felt chrismon or symbol that represented the statement and hung it on the felt tree. We talked about Jesus being the bread of life, and Sally made a loaf of bread. The next evening we talked about Jesus being the Good Shepherd, and Amy made a shepherd's staff. Sally made a door on the evening we learned that Jesus was the door of the sheep. Amy made a sun when we discussed Jesus as the light of the world. We made vines and branches and then a long, winding path to signify that Jesus was the way, the truth, and the life. We had trouble thinking of a symbol for the resurrection and the life. We finally decided on a cross with a smiling face above it.

It was not the conventional Christmas tree, but we did have

fun, and it provided much opportunity for learning. I planned it with the girls in mind, but Tom and I benefited greatly, especially when we were called upon by the girls to explain. "What does it mean, Daddy or Mama?" There's nothing like answering children's questions to make one think simply.

Just before going to Seattle, we went Christmas caroling. It was the perfect evening for it. As we bundled ourselves up in jackets, boots, mittens, scarves, and knitted caps, a light snow began to fall. We were glad to see it was snow. Last year our Christmas caroling spirit had literally been dampened by rain.

At the coffee shop we met the other people who were going caroling. Then we merrily piled into two trucks. Tom and the girls and I rode in the back of Babe's truck. We stopped at the Imuses' and sang for them. Then up the road again to sing for Paul. He was a precious old Swiss man in his eighties. He had lived many years in Stehekin and despite his many health problems continued to keep his photography shop and live at the head of the lake in his little cabin.

"Silent night, holy night. All is calm, all is bright, Round yon Virgin, mother and child," we sang as he stood quietly in the opened doorway. The light from inside shone on his smiling face. When we finished singing, he beckoned for us to wait as he stepped back into the house. In a moment he was shuffling toward us with his hands filled with oranges. Fresh fruit was a precious commodity in an area such as ours, with infrequent contact with the grocer. It was a real act of love for Paul to give us his oranges. It was hard to take them, but it would have been harder not to.

With a new feeling of the real spirit of Christmas we went on up the road, jostling and shivering and laughing and singing in the back of the open truck. The darkness, the gently falling snow, and the season made it safe for us to allow ourselves to share a comradeship that was not common in such a life as we were living.

Finally we came to our last stop. It was at the Courtneys' home. They lived nine miles from the landing in a rustic but lovely cabin they had built themselves. Ray's father had homesteaded in Stehekin years ago, and Ray and Esther still lived here with their five sons and one daughter. They were gracious and open people, and we always enjoyed visiting with them. This evening was no exception.

Their cabin was back a good distance from the road, as a huge pasture had been cleared for the horses they used in their back-country guide business. We parked in the turn-around at the end of the main road and walked on top of the snow, stepping easily over the fences because the snow level was already pretty high.

The girls raced ahead to see Peggy Ann and the boys. Tom and I walked leisurely hand in hand. It was too beautiful a night to rush. The light snow had stopped, and the moon was trying to find a hole in the clouds. When it did, there was a breathtaking scene of a river rushing along the base of tall, snow-covered mountains. We saw the door of the cabin open. A shaft of light fell across the porch. It seemed very bright against the black night. The figure of a tall man stood in the door. He raised his hand in greeting. We heard Ray's voice exclaim in a pleasant, surprised, welcome sort of way, "Well!"

As we began to sing "Joy to the world, the Lord is come," other figures came to the door and stepped out onto the porch. I was shivering with the cold from riding in the open truck and being outside for so long, but as I saw the skating moon silhouetting the mountains and the family on the porch silhouetted by the light from the door and listened to the voices singing with me, I was warm and mellow inside. It seemed that in fact at the moment "heaven and nature" were singing.

It was a beautiful preparation for the coming of the Christ Child.

11

Swirling snow filled the January night. The wind threw snow at the windows of our cabin. But we were cozy and secure by the fireplace. We enjoyed a simple but delicious meal with our cousin, Edith. After she had come to visit us the first fall we were in Stehekin, she had come back the next summer to live and work. She was an excellent cook, and the lodge customers were grateful for her expertise. Edith's grandmother and Tom's grandmother had been sisters. That made Edith a distant relative, but because of sharing our lives so closely for three years, Edith was really our sister. She spent many hours with us at home and on the mountain trail. She prepared many meals for us and sewed innumerable stitches into the quilt that waited for attention in its frame by the fireplace. Who knows how many stories she read to Sally and Amy or how many walks she took with them. And how they loved going to her cabin to stay overnight and be indulged in a way that never happens at one's own home. I thanked the Lord many times for sending Edith to us.

This particular blizzardy January evening Edith had made dinner for us at our house. We had washed dishes and children, and Edith was reading the bedtime story while I listened and worked on the mittens I was knitting for Sally. Tom came out of the bathroom and called me. He went back into the bathroom, and I followed.

One look at his face and I knew something was dreadfully wrong.

"Look at that," he said, pointing into the toilet. The water was red.

"What is it?" I asked.

"Urine."

"Urine?" I looked at it again. It looked more like cherry Kool-Aid. "Yours?"

He nodded.

"Dear God," I whispered.

In the silence we could hear Edith and the girls laughing over their story in the living room.

I suddenly felt as though I was not really in this bathroom but rather a spectator of the whole scene. I could see the woman and two little girls in the living room snuggled together in front of the fireplace, giggling over the pictures in a book. I could see a man and woman standing dumbly in a bathroom, staring at each other's white faces. I could see that man as a little boy of five years telling his mommy exactly what he had just told his wife. I knew that little boy had come within a hair of death because of this very same problem. He had lived only because his father, a physician, had not been willing to give up and had instead tried an experimental procedure. The child had lived and was now this man reliving that same dreadful moment of discovering his urine was really blood.

I heard the woman in the bathroom say to her husband, "We need to get you to a doctor right away."

The man pulled back the curtain from the window, and the light streamed out. Snow swirled angrily about the window.

Suddenly I was no longer a spectator. The dryness of my lips, the tightness in my throat, and the pounding of my heart made the scene real. I took Tom's hand. It was cold.

"There's no way I can get out of the valley tonight," Tom said flatly. "Ernie can't fly in the dark, and the sheriff's boat can't make it up the lake in this storm."

As he spoke, fear grew in me until it possessed me completely.

I reached for Tom, and as we stood clinging to each other, I began to pray silently, "Jesus, dear Jesus. Help us. Please help us."

Immediately I felt the fear begin to drain away and I began to think more clearly.

"We'll get you out as soon as we can tomorrow. The doctor will want a specimen. I'll go get a little jar."

When I returned from the storeroom with a jar, Tom was sitting limply on the side of the bathtub.

Handing him the jar, I said, "Edith can stay with the girls, and I'll go with you to the doctor."

"Then who will teach?" Tom asked simply. "You're the only substitute in the valley. You'll have to stay here and keep school."

Three years after Tom and I had been married, I had had kidney surgery. I knew the tests that would be done on Tom, and I knew how painful they were. I wanted to be with him.

"Look. We could close school for the day and make it up later," I suggested.

"No. You stay here. I'll be okay."

After I helped Edith tuck the girls in bed, I said to her, "Let's start back to the landing now. The way it's snowing, it may take a while."

I said good-bye to Tom and assured him we'd get him out tomorrow. "When I take Edith back to her cabin by the lodge, I'll have someone radio Ernie and make arrangements for him to come after you tomorrow."

"Be careful driving, Sweetie Pie," he said, using the name for me that he had used in the early days of our marriage. He had used it seldom in the last few years. His use of it now betrayed to me his emotions.

The five-mile trip took us half an hour. The snow blew across the road and flung itself into the headlights. It piled up on the windshield wipers and deepened on the road. I drove as quickly as I dared. Most of the way I talked to Jesus, asking for His help and guidance. I asked Him to keep the road open till I got back home. I also prayed that the storm would stop so that Tom could get out of the valley at daylight.

As we neared the landing area, I said to Edith, "Do you have a key to the office? I need to call Ernie." I could feel Edith's eyes on me in the dark.

"I thought something was wrong," she said quietly. "What is it?"

"Tom is urinating blood." The words ripped at my throat as they came out. Tears began to sting my eyes. I could barely hear Edith's, "Oh no!"

Everything was quiet except for the wind, the hum of the motor, and my sniffing.

Finally Edith said, "I don't have a key tonight, since I don't open the lodge tomorrow morning. But Maxine will have a key to the kitchen. There's a radio there, too."

We parked at the landing, and leaning into the wind, we walked to Maxine's cabin. She was ready for bed but dressed quickly and went with us to try to make radio contact.

"KOA801 Lodge calling KPB22." Again and again she called, and silence was the only response.

I waited until I was afraid to wait any longer, for snow was piling up rapidly and I had to drive home alone.

"I'll come back first thing in the morning," I said. "If I can get here," my mind added. I pulled on my hood and mittens and opened the door.

"I'll keep trying to get Ernie, and I'll be praying for you and Tom," Maxine said quietly.

"So will I," added Edith.

I looked into their eyes and saw a deep caring. "Thank you," I said, grateful for their concern.

The drive home was long, but it gave me plenty of time to pour out my fears to the Lord. By the time I got home, I was able to greet Tom with a smile.

"How are you now?" I asked, hanging my snowy coat near the fire to dry and sitting down next to him.

"I feel all right, but nothing has changed. Did you get hold of Ernie?"

"No. There was no answer."

He turned and looked at the fire. "I'm not surprised. Why would he stay near the radio on a night like this?"

"I'll go down first thing in the morning and see if we can get hold of him. Maxine said she'd keep trying."

"So all we can do is wait." He sighed and leaned his head back on the couch.

"Yes, but we can pray, too." Tom and I had never prayed together, just the two of us. A great desire to pray with him swelled up in me. "Tom, let's pray together."

I moved closer to him. He took my hand tightly in his, and his eyes searched mine. I felt his eyes probing mine. "What is he looking for?" I wondered. For a moment time was suspended. It seemed the world stopped while this man looked into his wife's eyes.

"Jesus," I thought, "let him find what he's looking for."

Then the moment passed, and he bowed his head and prayed simply, "Lord, we need You. There is nothing we can do. We are literally helpless. So, Lord, we just give everything to You and ask You to please help us through the night. Thank You. Amen."

We sat together, holding hands and gazing at the fire. A quietness filled the little cabin, and as time slipped away, we simply waited for the night to pass. After some time Tom turned to me and said, "We might as well go to bed. There's no need to sit up all night."

The next morning we were up before daylight. As I set the fire in the fireplace, Tom came to me with another little jar and a smile. The liquid in the jar was yellow, with only a faint reddish cast. I jumped up from in front of the fire. As I clung to him, tears slid down my nose.

"Thank You, Jesus," I whispered.

"Your fire is about to go out," Tom said with a smile.

I turned and looked at the smoking kindling. "Oh no," I groaned. Tom gently pushed me aside and poked here and there in the fire, and instantly flames leaped up.

I sat beside him on the couch as he pulled on his boots.

"I still think you need to go downlake to the doctor," I said.

"I probably should," he agreed, pulling at the laces.

I thought again of the uncomfortable tests he would have to go through. I decided not to tell him about them for fear he would not go to the doctor.

When he finished with the boots, he put his hand on my knee and said, "Let's pray again."

I was surprised and delighted, and it was my turn to search his eyes. I saw peace and gratitude glowing in those deep brown eyes. We both understood there seemed to be great power in our prayers offered together.

Tom bowed and prayed quietly, as though talking to a friend, "Thank You, Lord, for making me better this morning. We feel I should still go to the doctor. We just put this whole thing in Your hands and ask You to be with us today, with me at the doctor's, and with Lois as she teaches for me. I ask You to help her with all those kids. Thank You, Lord, for hearing us. Amen."

Once more I began to feel tears stinging my eyes as I looked at my husband. I had been asking the Lord for weeks to bring Tom to Him. My prayer was being answered. I knew I was seeing the beginning of a beginning.

By the time school started, I had taken Tom to the lodge to wait for word from Ernie. It was still snowing but very lightly. Maxine had contacted Ernie, and he said he would come as soon as he could get the snow off the wings and as soon as it got warmer, so that the wings would not ice up. We realized that might not happen for some time, but Tom decided to stay at the lodge and wait. The girls and I went back to the school and got ready for the day there.

By the time I had the fire going there, the children were beginning to arrive. I was quickly absorbed in giving out lessons to ten children in six different grades, one through eight. When everything was organized, or as much as could be expected, I began the reading lessons with the two youngest. Then there was a constant parade of people with questions. It required a quick changing of gears as the different children doing their own lessons asked different questions. "Mrs. Olson, when I check this multiplication problem like the book says to do, it doesn't come out right. What's wrong with it?" "Mrs. Olson, where is Belgium on the map?" "Mrs. Olson, Eric took my eraser. Make him give it back." "Mrs. Olson, how do you spell *unnecessary?*" "Mrs. Olson, is *fairly* an adverb or an adjective?" "Mrs. Olson, are black spiders poisonous? Because there's one crawling on your shoulder." "Mrs. Olson, I'm cold. The fire went out."

There was not much time for me to think about Tom. Shortly after lunch a truck stopped in front of the school. Babe got out, and I met him at the door.

"Tom wanted me to tell you that he left about half an hour ago with Ernie. There was trouble with the wings icing up, so Ernie just made it a while ago. Tom said he probably won't be back tonight. Is there anything I can do to help you?"

"Thanks for coming to tell me." I smiled gratefully. "Yes, there is something you can do. Would you please cut some more wood for the fire tomorrow? We are about to use up what's here."

When school was over, the mother who had kept Amy for me brought her back to school. She graciously agreed to keep Amy the next day while I kept school for Tom. The girls and I went home. The house was cold. It seemed as though I was constantly building fires these last few days.

I was glad to go to bed that night. I crawled under the quilts and closed my eyes. The bed seemed cold and empty without Tom. I wondered how he was feeling tonight. I wished I could be with him. I knew that he was probably still in pain from the tests. I wondered what the doctors had found out. If there were only telephones here, I could talk to him. But there wasn't, so I talked to Jesus and asked Him to talk to Tom for me and comfort him and keep him from feeling alone in the night. All at once I didn't feel alone either. I slept soundly and restfully.

The next morning dawned bright and clear. School went well, and I was waiting at the lodge when word came that Ernie was on his way, bringing Tom home. I watched as Tom walked painfully from the plane to the lodge with Ernie's help.

I met them on the steps. "Are you all right?" I asked.

Ernie's slow grin broke across his face. "He's had quite a time down in the city. You'd better take care of him."

He helped Tom into the car as I rounded up the girls, and we headed home. "What did they say?" I asked him.

"They couldn't find anything wrong. Thanks to the Lord there seemed to be no reason for the bleeding. Everything is fine now except, do I ever hurt."

"Thank You, Jesus," I said aloud. Then I added silently, "And thank You that he is thanking You, too."

12

The second winter was hard. We all had a bout with the flu. Then I got cystitis and had to go out to the doctor. There was about twice as much snow as the winter before. I began to feel as though I was a rabbit living in a hole in the ground. Snow was piled to the eaves of the house, and more snow was waiting to slide off the roof if it only had someplace to fall. For a while we couldn't even use the front door because there was too much snow. We had to crawl over the wood stored on the side porch to get out. The novelty of a wilderness winter wore off. I began to suffer from cabin fever. I was so anxious to see someone that whenever I heard a car or truck motor, I jumped up on a chair to look out. The snow was so high I could not see out otherwise. Tom shoveled the snow away from the windows, but that only relieved the pressure of weight on the window. I still couldn't see because of the snowbank.

I wrote cantankerous letters to my friends in Ohio. I was thoroughly annoyed at what I judged to be their complacent attitudes toward life. I viewed their satisfaction with simply discussing life as just plain chicken. I thought they should go out and risk it instead. Yes, do something daring, like we had done. Experience some real trials. Dare to find out what they were made of. I made a tape and sent it to them. It came back with Jolene saying, "Lois, I can't bear to hear you talk like that. I'm not even going to answer you. Don't be so hard on yourself and us. Just because we are in a different pie doesn't mean there are no pits in it."

I was stricken and totally ashamed. I recognized my own problem. Yes we had dared and risked a great deal. Yes we had learned an enormous amount about ourselves, our strengths and weaknesses. God in His wisdom knew how He must make us grow. But not every one needed to go through the same experiences to grow. I was overwhelmed with my false pride. In tears and true humility I confessed, as David had done, "Have mercy upon me, O God, according to thy lovingkindness. . . . For I acknowledge my transgressions: and my sin is ever before me. Against thee, thee only, have I sinned. . . . Create in me a clean heart, O God; and renew a right spirit within me" (Ps. 51:1, 3-4, 10).

The community gatherings took on a new meaning for me. I no longer attended them as quaint examples of mountain life. Instead they became my real contact with people. One day a week the ladies got together. We talked, shared recipes, and worked on a project. Sometimes they were individual projects. Other times we worked on one project. That's when I learned to quilt. There was great community and togetherness in sitting around a quilt frame, sharing life and actually sewing our lives together in the quilt. I treasure my quilt, not just because the top was made as a wedding present for my parents (it was never quilted, and Mother gave it to me before we left Ohio), but because it represents so much giving of other people to me. We did not talk about the same things that my city friends and I had talked about. We did not discuss books and the latest research studies, as we often had in Ohio. But there was a real feeling of giving of what one had and yet a shyness, too, for seldom was anything given that had not first been asked for.

The Saturday night square dances were great fun. Rebecca's parents started those. Her mother patiently taught us to square dance. We seldom had more than two squares, and usually that required some of the children's participation, but we did have a grand time. The community hall was chilly, even with the barrel stove going, and steam rose off the men's backs. We learned to do-si-do and promenade home. We laughed and stumbled and messed up the squares. At the end of the evenings we stomped over the snow, bound for home with a new sense of belonging and sharing.

Potlucks were called for any reason, from important ones such as graduation from the school to "let's have a get-together." The food was always terrific and ample. After the meals we talked or played games if our chief game leader, Mrs. Bowles, was there. The children ran, chased, shouted, hid, and played all the rowdy outside games children play.

One of our favorite community fun times was movie night. Someone ordered a film and we tromped through the snow to the community hall, now turned into a theater. Someone always brought big grocery bags full of popcorn, and we passed the popcorn while we watched the movies. Between reels, we passed a can. It was for money to pay for the rental of the film. If enough money had not been collected on the first round, the can was passed again until the needed amount was received. If too much was collected, it was saved toward the next film. The best part about the movies was the audience. We seldom got first-rate movies because of the expense involved. The movies were sometimes rather silly, and the audience made the most of it. There was a constant dialogue going on between film and viewers. Often the actors' lines were never even heard because of the substitutions of the crowd between mouthfuls of munching popcorn. I always thought our lines were much funnier than the scripts. These evenings were always hilarious, and they made me forget I lived in a snow cave.

The Bible studies continued to be a big lift for me. We not only had a great sense of community, but we also had fellowship in the Lord. There was more depth and reason for our being together.

There were also times that unexpected visitors came to our house. Usually they were people who were cross-country skiing on the airstrip, which made a much better ski field than an airstrip. Our house was the nearest cabin to the airstrip, and often we would have people knocking on our door, asking if they could come in to warm up their skis to change the wax. Cold wax just does not go on cold skis very well. They were almost always valley people, so we never minded. But occasionally they were tourists staying at the lodge for a skiing holiday. Then I would sometimes be embarrassed by our comfortable home, with games and projects and laundry racks scattered all around. Finally I decided that I had been embarrassed for the last time. I vowed never again to put the drying rack next to the fire. I would leave it in the bathroom even if it did take three days for the clothes to dry in there.

Then one Sunday I had to break my resolution. The clothes were not getting dry in the bathroom, and we would need them for school the next day. I had to bring the drying rack out into the living room by the fire. No sooner did I get it in the living room than there was a knock at the door. "I hope it's a valley person," I thought as I answered the knock.

It wasn't. It was a very dignified-looking older couple.

"Good morning, ma'am," the gentleman said. "Would you mind awfully if we came in to warm our skis? We need to change the wax, you see."

They were not only nonvalley people; they were obviously English. Trying not to show my dismay, I invited them in. They stomped their feet to get the snow off and stepped in. While the gentleman went straight to the fireplace, the lady surveyed the kitchen and living room, which were equally visible. I followed her eyes and saw bread rising too high over the side of the big bread bowl. Rats! With the laundry, I'd forgotten to knead it again and get it in the pans. The breakfast dishes were stacked by the sink. Amy's house slippers were in the middle of the table next to the butter that had never gotten back in the refrigerator. The lady smiled and looked into the living room. It was a total wreck. Toys and books were everywhere. Mittens and caps were draped around the stone behind the Franklin stove. To top it off, there hung my panties and bra with the rest of the laundry.

"May I get you something warm to drink?" I asked quickly to divert her attention.

"That would be lovely. Thank you," she answered.

"Okay. You go ahead and sit down, and I'll—" I stopped because I realized she would have a problem finding a place to sit down. I started toward the couch to clear a place.

"Oh, don't bother, dear," she said. "It's all right."

Her voice was so calm and friendly. I looked at her in amazement.

"I don't mind," she said. "You have such a lovely home. I like it very much."

I saw that she meant it. I began to relax. We had a delightful conversation while her husband fixed the skis, and we all had tea. When they left, I remarked to Tom what a nice couple they were. He agreed.

"I loved to hear them talk. I say, don't you think they were marvelous?" I imitated their accent. "Wonder why they were here?"

"On a 'oliday, my dear." His accent was perfect.

"Wonder what kind of work he does?"

"He's the British consul general," Tom replied.

It was as though he had dropped a bomb.

"Do you mean to tell me that we have just entertained the British consul general and his wife with my underwear hanging right here for all the world to see?"

For a fact I never brought my underwear back into the living room to dry! But it really didn't matter. No one like the British consul general ever came to visit again.

13

It was my turn to go. I kissed the pajama-clad little girls and their handsome father and drove off toward Edith's cabin. It was my night to go alone to the Bible study. It was early spring. The snow was melting, but we hadn't reached the mud problem yet. The nights were still pretty cold, and I was glad for my heavy coat. The hot tea Edith shoved into my hand tasted good after the walk up the hill to her cabin.

There was a small group tonight, only five of us. We talked a few minutes and then got down to the study. John, Chapter 9, the healing of the man born blind. I was eager to talk about this Scripture. The Disciples had asked Jesus who had sinned, the man or his parents, so that the man was born blind. I understood that big question. Who knows how many times I'd asked myself that. In some moment of pain or distress over my limitations or some dark night of disappointment I cried out, "Why? Why, Lord, is my body like this?"

In junior high I had struggled especially hard with the effects that childhood polio had caused. I was very sensitive about my looking different because of a severe scoliosis and an atrophied right leg. I didn't want anyone to know I wore a back brace. I despised buying clothes because I was forced to look at myself and see that nothing looked right on me. Few people would have guessed that this caused me trauma. I didn't let on. I was popular at school and was active to my limit. I was student council president in junior high. In senior high I was the yearbook editor, along with being the state president of the Future Nurses Association. But even though I did not show the pain, it was very real to me, both physically and emotionally.

The most devastating thing happened when I was at a junior high church camp. I don't remember how it happened. I only carry a picture of a group of young people rocking in wicker chairs on a wide porch during a quiet afternoon break in activities. I was one of those children. A man was talking with us. He said to me, "Lois, you are crippled because you sinned against God. You are being punished justly for your sin."

A thousand knives run through me would not have hurt more than that man's misguided statement. I remember running as best I could to my bunk and sobbing in agony. What could I possibly have done to God to deserve the years of pain that I'd had? And not only my pain, but my parents and my sister and brother had suffered because of it. Why? Why would God do that? What had I done?

When I got home from camp and told my parents, they were enraged. "What a horrible thing to say to a child! How dare the man say that to you! It's not true! It's not true! Don't you believe it."

But if I didn't believe it, what could I believe? There was no answer for why.

The question surfaced at various times in my life. I had not dealt with it for some time. I did not even think of it now that I was secure in my love with Tom and our children. In my new relationship with God I did not consider it. I knew beyond a doubt that God loved me. Repeatedly He gave me assurances of His caring for me. I could no longer believe that He had stricken me to punish me. I understood that Jesus had taken the judgment of my sin unto Himself on the cross. I was counted as righteous in God's sight, so how could He punish me? I had loved the Lord as a child in my childish way and had known even then that He cared for me.

But the old question came back. Why? Why did I have these pains and limitations when others did not? I understood in my head that God was not punishing me, but perhaps my heart was not sure.

My winter of struggle had caused the question to rise to the surface. Later I realized that God in His loving wisdom knew that this would be a block in our relationship if it was not removed. Without my realizing it, He set about removing that deep hurt. It began at the Bible study that night.

We read together the story of Jesus healing the man born blind. We talked about where it happened, how it happened, what the Disciples learned from it, how the Pharisees felt about it, how the man's parents felt, and even how the man himself reacted. It was all very interesting and enlightening. I tried to keep the whole incident at a distance, in the intellect, where I could handle it. But God would not allow it.

Suddenly I blurted out, "But why? Why was this man born blind? Did he sin before he was even born? Did his mother and father sin? Then why punish the child for the parents' problem? I don't understand. Will somebody please tell me?"

But before anyone could answer me, I began to tell them, with deep emotion, what had happened to me at that camp. When I finished, the room was quiet. Then Babe reached over and touched my knee.

"Lois," he said gently. "Look at your Bible. Look at verse three. Read how Jesus answered that question."

Through my tears I read, "Jesus answered, 'His blindness has nothing to do with his sins or his parents' sins. He is blind so that God's power might be seen at work in him,'" (Good News Bible).

I looked up at Babe.

"For God's glory, Lois. This man was blind for God's glory. Maybe that's why you've suffered so much. God has a reason, even if you don't know it."

I was beginning to understand.

14

Winter seemed to have had its say. Spring was beginning to push into winter's territory. With the days becoming warmer, the sap began to flow in the trees. That meant one thing: maple syrup. In the glaring, glorious sunshine we tapped several trees and hung three-pound Crisco cans to catch the sap. Two or three times a day Amy and I made the rounds, emptying the buckets of sap into a large pail. What a joyous chore it was, walking in the sun, listening to the few early bird arrivals or those who had wintered with us, seeing the clearness in the sky, and feeling the hope and promise that spring always brings. Amy loved wading through the softening snow. Numerous times each trip I would have to stop and pull her out of a waist-deep hole. It became a hilarious game to her. Somehow the sap was gathered.

In the house she and I kneaded bread and went about other daily chores while the sap boiled slowly on the stove. The windows fogged up with the steam, and it was hard to see out, but Amy loved this, too. The windows became great playmates, with an endless opportunity to draw stick people with huge heads and smiling faces.

We also spent long, happy moments poring over the seed catalogs, deciding what plants we would have in the gardens this year. The doe who came around our cabin began to take on a plumper appearance. Everywhere there was promise of new life.

With this awakening electrifying the air, my prayers for Tom increased. Again and again I asked that the Lord would bring new life to Tom, that somehow Tom would see with his heart who

Jesus really was and then commit his life to the Lord. I loved Tom deeply, and he was a wonderful, loving man with many talents. But I kept saying to myself and the Lord, "Just think what he could be with God as his source and strength!" I was excited about his steps toward God, his interest in the Bible, his questions about its meaning for him, his newfound belief in prayer. It was almost as if there was a new sap beginning to rise in Tom, giving him new life and growth. I prayed for it daily and anticipated its happening.

Tom has always had a weakness and still does to this day. He loves to lie down, pull up his shirt, and have his back lightly scratched. He will do almost anything to have his back scratched, especially just before he goes to sleep. I would rather go to sleep reading a good book. Tom was not overly interested in reading, especially at night, but I enjoyed it. I read so many things that I thought he should read, and it was a small source of irritation to me that he seldom read what I suggested. So after eleven years of marriage we found the perfect solution. Every evening we got into bed, turning off all lights except the reading lamp on my side of the bed. Tom pulled up his shirt, and I scratched his back while he listened to me read aloud to him. It was a perfect arrangement, but there was one flaw. He always went to sleep at the best part of the story. It infuriated me.

"You're asleep!" I'd yell.

"No I'm not," came a muffled, garbled voice.

"Then why were you snoring?" I'd demand.

"I wasn't snoring," came the same unconvincing voice.

"All right, then tell me what I just read to you," I'd test him.

"Well—" and he'd raise himself up on his elbows, blink his bleary eyes, and tell me something.

"That was five pages ago!" I'd storm.

"Sorry," he'd say and then reach over and give me an especially loving kiss. That always melted my frustration and resistance. "I loved the back scratch," he'd say with a twinkle in his eyes. Then he'd reach over and turn out the lamp, and so ended that reading session.

Progress was pretty slow as far as getting through books was concerned. But we did complete a number of them. One that had special meaning to us was Larry Christianson's *The Christian Family*. In this very readable book the Reverend Dr. Christianson details what a Christian family is all about, how it is different from other families, how each member functions in the family. We felt it really made sense. Shortly after we had completed the book, the topic came up in our weekly Bible study group. Tom was sharing some of the things from the book, and because the group was in our home that night, I was able to add my understanding of it.

"That sounds a lot like Bill Gothard's seminar," Maria Byrd said.

"Who's Bill Gothard?" Tom asked.

Maria explained to him briefly about Bill Gothard's Basic Youth Conflicts Seminar, which she had attended in Seattle the year before. She shared Mr. Gothard's understanding of what the Bible has to say about family structure and authority. She told how meaningful the seminar had been for her and what spiritual growth it had fostered in her. When she finished, Tom said, "That sounds like something I'd like to go to." I looked at him quickly because I was shocked he'd said that. The expression on his face showed that he was equally amazed. Afterward he told me he was so surprised that he wanted to look around to see who said it. But Maria was excited.

"Oh I think you would really like it. These seminars are given all over the country, so he is here only once or twice a year. But I think there will be another one this spring sometime. I'll find out and let you know."

The next time we saw Maria, she gave us a brochure and an application blank for the next Seattle seminar, which was to be held at the end of May. We read that it was a week-long session, with Monday through Thursday nights and all day Friday and Saturday. The cost was forty-five dollars, including the large notebook of materials. Tom sat right down and filled out the application. Then as he wrote the check, he said to me, "I can't believe I'm doing this. A week away from work plus forty-five dollars is a lot to pay for a seminar. At least I can stay with my sister."

When the time came, it was with great excitement and anticipation that I waved good-bye to him on the ferry and returned to keep school while he was gone. My prayers for him increased as the week passed.

The next Sunday afternoon a friend's car stopped in front of our cabin. Tom got out, waved to the friend, and turned toward our cabin, carrying his suitcase and a grocery sack. The moment I saw his face, I knew there was a difference in him. And it wasn't just his face. He even walked differently. There was a new, unhurried vitality in his step, a new confidence.

"Daddy's home," I called to the girls.

They ran from their room and out the door to meet him. They flung their arms around him. He put down the suitcase and sack and pulled them close to him. He very often hugged them, but this time there was something different in the way he did it. Was it with more tenderness? He kissed them with great joy and yet such gentleness. He pulled them to him as though they were the most valuable treasures in the world, and yet there was no possessiveness in his action.

"What'd you bring us, Daddy?" Amy asked, freeing herself from his embrace and looking in the sack. "Bananas! Apples!" she shouted, jumping up and down.

I joined the little group, and Tom embraced me. I expected a kiss, but instead he looked at me with—what was it in his eyes? Something flowed out of them to me. Love, yes, but it was not any love that I'd ever seen there before. "What is this?" I wondered. "What has happened to him?"

A slow smile came across his face. "I missed you," he said. "It was a wonderful experience. I can't wait to tell you about it."

The girls made a second attack on him, yelling thanks for the fresh fruit and pulling him toward the garden to see the little plants we'd set out while he was gone.

We had a noisy and joyful dinner that evening. After the girls had been properly tucked in by Daddy and his usual songs, Tom and I sat on the floor in front of the fire.

"Tell me about it," I said. "I can see something wonderful happened. You're so different."

"I am?" He seemed surprised. "How?"

"Well, I don't know exactly how to describe it. But you're just different, that's all. Tell me what the seminar was like."

"You know, when I got that brochure in the mail that listed all the sessions, I wondered if I could get through them all. I was sure I would get bored and would spend half the time doodling. I'd had hundreds of college and graduate school classes that were so dull I just couldn't see how a whole week, hour after hour, could be interesting. But the first night after I saw thousands of people in that coliseum, I thought, 'Maybe this guy is pretty good if this many people are coming to hear him.' After he got started, my whole attention was centered on every word he said. I'd never heard anyone talk like he did or say the things he was saying. In what seemed like five minutes, the whole evening was gone. Every session was like that. I couldn't wait to get there. Then on Thursday night he was talking about a passage in the Good News Bible version of Revelation where it says, 'I know what you have done; I know that you are neither cold nor hot. How I wish you were either one or the other! But because you are lukewarm, neither hot nor cold, I am going to spit you out of my mouth!' That really hit me. The Holy Spirit was convicting me. Suddenly I knew I was about the most lukewarm person I'd ever met and I knew I needed to make a decision. I had to decide one way or the other, either yes or no.

"Friday, during the evening session, we stood to sing a song. That coliseum was packed, and every person was singing."

His eyes closed, and he began to sing softly:

> *Oh Lord my God! When I in awesome wonder*
> *Consider all the worlds* Thy hands have made,*
> *I see the stars, I hear the rolling* thunder,*
> *Thy power throughout the universe displayed,*
> *Then sings my soul, my Savior God to Thee:*
> *How great Thou art, how great Thou art!*
> *Then sings my soul, my Savior God to Thee:*
> *How great Thou art, how great Thou art!*

Tears filled my eyes as he sang the second verse about woods and forests, birds singing in trees, lofty mountains, brooks, and gentle breezes.

When he began the third verse, his voice began to tremble.

And when I think that God, His Son not sparing,
Sent Him to die, I scarce can take it in;
That on the cross, my burden gladly bearing,
He bled and died to take away my sin;

Tears streamed down his face as he sang,

Then sings my soul, my Savior God to Thee:
How great Thou art, how great Thou art!

He bent forward, and resting his head on his drawn-up knees, he began to weep. I had seen him cry only once before, as a result of a family loss. That had been great, choking sobs of grief. But this was different. He wept and wept, and as he wept, I felt no need to comfort him. He was being cleansed. A lifetime of buried guilt, anxiety, mistrust, estrangement from God was welling up and flowing out.

As he cried, I cried tears of gratitude and praise. "Thank You, Father. Thank You, Jesus. Thank You, Holy Spirit."

Later that evening, as I lay in his arms, he said, "You know what else happened? Besides giving myself to the Lord, I gave you and the girls to Him. You don't belong to me. You belong to Him. We are a family knitted together by His love, but we belong to Him."

As the weeks passed, Tom showed us what he meant. He assumed the role of spiritual leader in our home. He read to us from the Bible and led us in daily devotions. We began to have a special little worship service on Sunday mornings. We sang hymns, and he read from a book of sermons for children.

There was a new, quiet assurance about him, a calmness I had never seen before. He was more open to others. He smiled easier and fuller, his delightful sense of humor was heightened, and how handsome he was! A new light, the light of Christ Jesus, was shining through his heart into our home.

Our joy was increased as I received a release from the Lord to share with Tom the exciting experiences that I had had in coming to the Lord. The "baby" I had been carrying was born.

15

The August sun felt warm on my lap as we jolted along the road to Cottonwood Camp. It was at the farthest end of the road, twenty miles from the boat dock. The upper eleven miles were passable only in summer after the snow had melted and the road crew had removed fallen trees and rocks and repaired washouts. It was always an adventure to drive to Cottonwood. We never knew what we would find in or along the road. The road was narrow, barely wide enough for a car at many points. My heart always beat a little faster as we crept along the edge of the rocks with barely more than a foot of road before the drop to the raging river. At other places the lush growth of bushes forced its way into the car windows on both sides and even reached across the top of the car. Bear and deer sightings were common along this road. One of the most exciting spots was a waterfall that swept over the rocks and down onto the road before tumbling into the river. What a thrill to drive right through the waterfall, hearing that roaring and pounding on the car roof!

This particular morning Tom and I were bouncing along, heading for the trail head at the end of the road. Our girls were spending the day with another valley family, and Tom and I were celebrating our twelfth wedding anniversary by hiking to Cascade Pass. This was a trip that Tom had made several times. He felt it was not particularly difficult and offered numerous spectacular views. I was a bit reluctant because of the distance of eleven miles. My longest hike in one day had been six miles, but that was with a backpack. Long periods of time on my feet caused quite se-

vere pain in my back and right hip and thigh due to back problems and paralysis of abdominal muscles and muscles in my right
leg. I had hesitated going on long hikes or ones that were at all
strenuous. But I had heard again and again how breathtakingly
beautiful the view was from the top. So I stuffed my appre-
hensions into the back of my mind and agreed to try for the top.

We parked the car in the turnaround at the end of the road
and paid a visit to the "last chance latrine." Throwing the heavy
jackets into the car, Tom shouldered the small day pack that held
our lunch, photographic supplies, and my sunglasses.

"The troops are ready, my dear Sacajawea," he said, bowing low.

"Right this way, Mr. Lewis. Or are you Mr. Clark?"

"Both," was the answer as he pulled my bandana backward and
trotted off down the path.

"Hold on now. I thought I was the guide," I called, running
after him and retying my scarf.

I couldn't see him ahead, so I stopped. "Mr. Lewis. Mr. Clark,"
I called.

Instantly something jumped at me from behind a large cottonwood tree. "You called, dear?" Tom said as he bowed again.

As I recovered from the suddenness of his reappearance, we
laughed heartily and started up the trail hand in hand.

Soon the trail narrowed, and we had to walk in single file. In
the brushy areas Tom went first, holding back the branches for
me to pass. Then the trail began to climb gently as we left the valley floor. My pace slackened slightly, and I began to breathe
faster.

Later I stopped to rest. "How much farther to the rockslide?" I
asked.

"Not very far," Tom answered.

I remembered the slide as a gigantic obstacle when we had
brought the schoolchildren on a day's outing the first fall we were
in the valley. We had gone to Horseshoe Basin, a spectacular gla-
cial cirque with at least a dozen waterfalls. The trail to Horseshoe
Basin, which took off from this trail to Cascade Pass, was only
two and one-half miles from the trail head.

We came to the avalanche of rocks and boulders and began to

pick our way over the enormous pile. I felt like an ant in a gravel pit. Halfway across the rocky expanse I stopped my half crawl, half walk and took off my flannel shirt. We had learned early in our wilderness experience to dress in layers, and now the cool air felt refreshing on my neck and bare arms. I tied the shirt around my waist and crawled on, the sun getting warmer and warmer on my back.

At last we reached the other side, and Tom caught me as I jumped down from the last big rock.

"Phew!" I sighed. "That's work. How much farther to water?"

"Basin Creek is just ahead. We can sit down a second and catch our breath, too," Tom said, but I noticed he was not puffing. A vague feeling of doubt poked its way into my thoughts. I was already feeling the stress, but Tom showed no sign of it.

We walked on to Basin Creek. We could hear it long before we saw it. It was splashing and tumbling along over rocks, coming from snowmelt higher in the mountains and hurrying on in the Stehekin River. I sat down on a rock next to the creek while Tom dipped the sierra cup into the cold stream.

"It's pretty cold," he said as he handed it to me. "Drink it slowly."

Cold was hardly the word for it. Instantly my teeth ached, and my lips tingled, but how delicious it tasted. How refreshing it was to my dry throat.

I got up from the rock and stooped by the creek. I splashed the freezing water over my arms and felt the pleasant shock of the water on my hot face.

"Pardon me, Miss Sacajawea, but are we on a bathing expedition or a hiking expedition?" came Tom's most exaggerated gentleman voice.

"Both, sir," I answered in my fakest aristocratic voice. I swooped my cup through the water and flung its contents at Tom.

"Hey!" came the surprised response to my perfect aim.

I dashed to the log that crossed the stream, but a couple of steps out and I was forced to forget the yells and splashes behind me. I had to concentrate on balancing my way across this log.

Shortly after we were on a firm, if rocky, path again, we came to some abandoned rusty mining equipment lying in a flat, open area near what looked like the foundation of a small cabin. I remembered seeing it before on the trip to Horseshoe Basin and recalled Tom's explanation. There had once been an active mine in the basin. That's how the road came to be built. However, the Black Warrior Mine was short-lived because its produce was not long able to exceed the cost and trouble of getting the ore out.

As we went on up the trail, I was quiet, thinking of all I had heard about the Black Warrior Mine. It was astounding to me that two thousand people could have lived at the area now called Bridge Creek Camp Ground, about eleven miles down from where we were. We had poked through two old buildings still standing there, but it was still hard to imagine. The difficulty of getting supplies in and the ore out must have been incredible. It made my cabin seem to be right downtown!

As I mused, I began to feel the intense heat of the sun. The trail was totally in the open, with no hope of shade. The vegetation was low bushes or leaves and stems from the earlier wild flowers. Presently we passed the fork to Horseshoe Basin, and the trail began to climb sharply. Immediately I began to feel the stress. Tom was well ahead of me. He found it difficult to go slowly on a steep path. I didn't really need his help, so I suggested he go ahead. Before he went in front of me, he gave me a package of gorp (trail food consisting of dried fruit and nuts). I had climbed little more than a quarter of a mile when I began to feel dizzy. The sun was unmercifully hot, and the trail seemed to me to be a vertical path. The pain was becoming more insistent. I stopped to rest and ate some of the gorp. I looked up at Tom on one of the switchbacks above me. He was waving his arms and calling, "Water here."

The memory of that cold, tingly water spurred me on up the switchbacks to where Tom was. A lovely waterfall was tumbling over the rocks into a swirling pool. The water fell from here into the creek that fed the river. Actually this was very near the source of the Stehekin River. I gratefully accepted the refreshing water and sat down on a large, hot rock.

"How are you feeling?" Tom asked.

"Fine," I fibbed.

"Is it too steep for you?"

"I can make it," I answered, almost snapping.

"We can stop any time you want," Tom offered. "We're out for the fun of it, not to set a record."

"I'm going to the top," I said sharply.

"Okay, but remember you have to go back the same distance you came."

It was a horrible thought and forced me to notice the pain that was now throbbing in my back and hip.

I took another drink and said, "Let's go."

"Want me to stay with you?" Tom asked, looking carefully at me.

"No, go ahead. I'm too slow for you."

He looked at me for a moment longer and then turned toward the switchbacks. He went on but did not get quite as far ahead as he had before.

Each step was becoming a struggle for me. I could not ignore the pain, and I was very hot. But I was not going to stop before I got to the top. A stirring of anger began to rise in me. I was a step beyond determination in my feelings and drive to get to the top.

At this point I saw some hikers coming toward me, two women, probably in their forties, and three young people. The youth passed me nearly running. One woman smiled kindly and said, "It's hard work, isn't it? Keep going and you'll make it." She went on past me, and then the second woman stopped.

"What's wrong with you?" she pounced on me. "Why are you going so slow? Why, this is hardly a morning's walk. Why, I've hiked *much* more difficult trails than this one. I'm just so strong I can climb anything, even something as steep as this," and she made an imaginary vertical path with her arm.

Anger flared in me. "Good for you," I said, not too nicely, I'm afraid. I was wishing that she were a fly on her vertical wall of a trail. I would have been happy to use a flyswatter on her.

Instead I directed my anger at the path and went a fair distance before I'd cooled off enough to feel the nagging ache in my back and hip. Two switchbacks later, the pain had moved down to my knee. I took one more step and knew that I could not go on. I was nearly paralyzed with the discomfort. I froze in that step, and defeat crushed me. Tears ran down my hot face.

"What kind of a softy are you?" I demanded of myself angrily through clinched teeth. "Why can't you go on? Don't you want to get to the top? Isn't that what you came to do? It can't be that much farther. If you had any guts at all, you could make it. But no. You're weak, weak, weak. All your life you've been a weakling. Aren't you sick of it? Go on. Be strong. Go to the top."

Resentment and bitterness poured out of me. Part of me was astonished, part of me seethed, and all of me wanted to scream. Instead I just stood there sobbing.

Who knows how long I stood there. Probably not very long. Tom came back down the switchbacks looking for me. When he saw me, he was aghast.

"Lois, what's wrong?" he demanded, taking hold of my shoulders.

"I can't make it," I sobbed. "I can't make it to the top. I've come all this way, and I can't make it."

Silently he put his arms gently around me and pulled me to his chest. But I didn't want comfort.

"Why do I have to be this way?" I demanded as I pushed away from him. "Why? Why have I always had a dumb old pain somewhere? Why have I always had to 'take it easy'?" I whined the last words in an imaginary nurse's tone. "Why have I always had to go home from school and go to bed for an hour instead of running and playing with my friends? Do you know I hated that so much I didn't want anyone to know I had to do it, so I told them I had been very bad and was being punished, and that's why I couldn't play with them? Why have I had to stand for hours in front of doctors, feeling like some strange specimen? Why have I always had every disease there was to have? Why, I want to know. Why me?" My anger was almost spent, and the next question came in a quiet, plaintive groan. "Why did God do this to me?"

The shock on Tom's face had turned to tenderness. "Oh, Lois," he said softly. He reached out and put his hand on the side of my head. His hand fell slowly and gently to my shoulder. Then he took my chin in his hand and lifted it so that he could look into my eyes.

"I don't know why you've had so much pain, but I do know that God loves you more dearly and tenderly than you'll ever know. Don't keep on looking at what you can't do and can't change. Think about all the good things God has given you."

For an instant he glanced over my head and into the distance. "Lois," he said quietly. "Do you know where you are? Turn around and look where you are."

He turned me by the shoulders, and there before me stretched the most beautiful scene I've ever witnessed. I had climbed high enough that it seemed I was nearly at the top of the world. Stretching out below me was a breathtakingly beautiful green, U-shaped valley with gigantic, rocky, jagged mountains along the sides. A stream flowed through the center of the valley, with little streams from the mountains joining it here and there. I had never seen such beauty.

A gentle, cool breeze brushed against my hot face as my heart absorbed the view. Fresh tears came, tears of repentance and, yes, tears of acceptance. Acceptance of myself just as I was, with no more questions asked. Joy and thanksgiving began to flow and wash away the anger and resentment.

As the tears flowed down my face, I spoke softly to God, "Thank You, Father, for making me just as You have. Thank You for every hurt and pain. I don't know why You've done it this way, but that's okay. You know. Forgive me for my bitterness and resentment. Thank You for bringing me up this steep struggle so that I could see myself and You more clearly. Thank You, Father, for loving me that much."

At last I understood that I didn't have to understand. It was enough that God loved me. He would tell me when I needed to know.

Tom hugged me gently, and we started down to the valley.

16

Summer passed quickly as we shared with more campers and visitors, and fished, hiked, and slept out under the stars. Fall tiptoed in quietly, and school began again. That September was magnificent. The colors were radiant. The clearness of the sky and air reflected the new clearness and brightness in our lives.

Amy and I went to school as usual. By now she was four and one-half years old. She still loved going to school while I taught. She especially enjoyed recess because that's when she could play with the children. She loved it when the bigger boys carried her on their shoulders or played games with her. The younger children liked to play hide-and-seek among the trees and rocks, and Amy always enjoyed that game.

On September ninth, during the lunch recess, Amy was sitting on a picnic table outside, watching the older children play baseball. One of the biggest boys was up at bat. Just as he began to swing at the ball, Amy jumped from the table and ran in front of him. It was too late for him to stop his swing. Instead of hitting the ball, his bat struck Amy's head. Amy fell to the ground in a little heap. The boy stood looking at her, too stunned to move. The boy who had been pitching ran to Amy and picked her up. Blood was dripping out of her ear. He carried Amy into the schoolhouse where I was. She was not really crying, just whimpering softly.

"Amy got hit by the bat," the boy gulped as he handed her to me.

Behind him stood the pale and shaking boy who had been

swinging the bat. As I numbly took Amy, I noticed the blood dripping out of her ear. That frightened me because I thought the blood was coming from inside her head and out of her ear. I knew that was a very dangerous sign.

Tom came in from where he had been with some other children. "Dear God, what happened?" he gasped. It was quickly explained to Tom as he grabbed Amy and ran to the car.

"Let's take her to Dr. Bowles," he said over his shoulder. Dr. Bowles was the retired doctor who lived in the valley from April until the middle of September. He hadn't left the valley yet, so we asked the older boys to take charge of the younger children, and we raced off to the doctor's cabin. Amy still was not crying. As a matter of fact, she was very quiet.

As Tom drove, I prayed, "Thank You, Lord, that Dr. Bowles is still here. Thank You for his skill. Please make him be at home." We stopped at their cabin and had carried Amy only halfway to the house when we saw Mrs. Bowles at the door. She disappeared into the cabin, and we heard her call, "Herbie, come quick. Something's happened to Amy."

She was back at the door when we got there. Herb was with her. He asked what had happened as we sat down. He gently inspected the wound area and found that the blood was not coming out of her ear but was, in fact, running down her head and dripping off the ear. He found a small cut about one inch long on the right side of her head. There was also a small bump. He carefully cleaned around the wound, clipping some of the hair out of the way, and put a bandage over the cut. I felt great gratitude to him for his gentleness and willingness to help us. We stayed with the Bowleses about half an hour, and Amy seemed all right. She was quiet but responsive. She seemed to use her body normally. She answered all our questions as she usually would except that she was a little more subdued than usual. So we decided that Tom should get back to the school and the doctor's wife would take Amy and me home. Dr. Bowles told us that if there was the slightest indication that anything was wrong, we should take her immediately down the lake to the hospital.

Mrs. Bowles, Amy, and I drove past the school, the falls, beside the river, over the bridge, and finally to the cabin where we lived.

"Are you sure you want me to leave you here?" Mrs. Bowles asked me.

I looked at Amy, and she looked normal. "Yes. We'll be all right. Tom will be home in a couple of hours."

"You don't have a car here," Mrs. Bowles reminded me.

"Yes I know," I said. "But Amy seems to be okay. It's just a bump on the head. She's had many bumps. We'll be fine. Thank you."

She drove away. I took Amy into the cabin and sat her on the couch. I got the small ice pack and put some ice in it. We laughed about Amy's funny cold hat on her head. Soon Amy began to look sleepy. I knew that I should not let her sleep, so I began reading to her. Then I asked if she would like to go to the bathroom. She said yes, so I carried her to the bathroom and unfastened her overalls. She sat down but did not support herself with her arms as she usually did. She began to fall to one side.

"Here, Amy," I said. "Put your arm here on the seat, and then you won't fall over."

She looked at me blankly and said, "What arm, Mommy?"

The first flash of alarm passed through me.

"This one," I said, and took hold of it. She looked at it as though she had never seen it before. I put it on the potty, and it bent like rubber, giving no support at all.

For the first time since we'd gone to Dr. Bowles, fear began to gnaw at my heart. Still I could not believe that anything was terribly wrong.

When she was finished, she stood up, and I said, "Why don't we take this bloody old shirt off and get a clean one instead?"

Amy followed me into the bedroom, and I got a shirt out of the drawer.

"Here, Amy, put your arms up, and let's pull that shirt off," I said.

One arm went up as usual. The left arm didn't move an inch. It just hung there, and her hand began to make a limp little fist.

A cold lump sat where my heart had been. I felt my throat begin to close. There was something dreadfully wrong with Amy,

and I was alone, without any help. From somewhere I heard a
voice that sounded like mine. It was talking very calmly. "Well
never mind, Amy. We'll just leave this shirt on."

I fastened her overalls and carried her to the couch.

"You sit here a minute," I said. "Here's your funny cold hat.
I'll go see what I can do."

My heart was racing. I was breathing quickly, but I felt no air
getting into my lungs. I went to the door and stepped out into the
sun. There was no one in sight in any direction. Our nearest
neighbor was over a mile away. I had no telephone to call for
help. There were no phones at all in the valley. I had no car to
drive her anywhere. A feeling of great tenderness for Amy swept
over me, followed by the icy reality that I was without human
help. Once more I turned to our "ever present help in time of
trouble." Psalm 50:15 came to me: "Call upon me in the day of
trouble: I will deliver thee, and thou shalt glorify me."

"O God," I cried out loud. "I am calling upon Thee, now.
Deliver us, please."

I went back inside. Amy was still on the couch. The ice pack
had slid down onto her shoulder, but she hadn't noticed. Her eyes
were glassy. Her left hand was in a tight fist, and out of the corner
of her mouth came a little stream of saliva.

"O my God," I whispered. "Help this precious child. There is
no one else who can. Please send us help for Amy."

Expecting to receive His help, I went back to the door. But still
no one was in sight. I went outside and called. No one answered.

An urgency filled me. "We could wait here for hours before
anyone comes by," I thought. "I must go somewhere where help
can find us."

I went back to Amy. "I don't know how far I can carry you," I
said to her, "but at least we'll be on our way, and if someone
comes, we can stop them."

She did not respond at all. I picked her up, ice pack and all,
and went out the door, closing it behind me. We started toward
the bridge. Amy weighed thirty-eight pounds. My back was injured from having had polio as a child. It would take the strength
of Jesus in me for me to be able to carry her even as far as the

bridge. As I walked, I prayed. "Dear God, I am walking out on Your promise. Psalm 37 says, 'The salvation of the righteous is of the Lord: he is their strength in the time of trouble. And the Lord shall help them, and deliver them.' Please, Lord, help us now. Send someone to help us."

I heard a funny sound, and I looked down. It was coming from Amy. She was trying to talk to me.

"Wha ah we ooing, Mommy?"

Her tongue rolled around in her mouth, and saliva trickled out the corner. Tenderness and pain and fear welled up in my throat, and for a minute I couldn't answer her. I had taught brain-injured children. I had seen their struggle to communicate. With agonizing sorrow I looked at my child and knew she was suffering from brain injury. As I carried her toward the bridge, it seemed as though the children I had taught walked beside us: Susan who could not speak, Terry who could walk only with great difficulty, LaVonn who had seizures, one after another. Tears flowed down my cheeks as I looked at my own child. She had always been so bright, so healthy and active. She talked well, even at a very early age. But now— "O God," I begged, "don't let her be changed from the beautiful, loving, healthy child she has always been. Please, Lord, don't let her have to endure the pain and struggle of those other children. Please send us help."

At that moment I heard a car. I stopped walking and looked in all directions. Then I saw it. It was coming from a service road near the bridge.

Thanksgiving and hope rose up in me.

"Stop!" I yelled. "Please stop! Please help us."

I tried to run, but I couldn't. Amy was too heavy for me. The car did not stop. It continued around a curve. I screamed again for it to stop, but I knew there was little chance I could be heard. The car would be on the bridge, and the roaring of the water would drown my call.

I felt Amy moving in my arms, and I saw that she was jerking and twitching. Her tongue clicked against the roof of her mouth, and her eyes were closed.

Desperation threatened to own me. "Jesus," I begged. "Please, Jesus." And the noise of the car stopped.

"Thank You, Jesus." I wept as I tried to run. I couldn't see the car, but I knew that it was just around the corner. If I could only get into its sight before it went on. But just then the car started up again. Despair came to live in me. I stopped my half run, half walk. "Jesus?" I asked. "What happened, Jesus?"

At that moment the car came into view, backing up. I saw the driver was a friend who lived farther up the valley. She backed the car to where I was and reached over and opened the door.

"Lois, what's wrong?" she asked. Her face reflected the concern in her voice.

"I've got to get Amy to the hospital somehow."

"Yes, I see you do," she said gently. "I wasn't sure I heard a call," she added as she started the car moving again. "I seldom come along here at this time of day. But I'm glad I did today."

So was I! "Thank You, Jesus."

As we raced around the corner and across the bridge and along the river, I briefly explained to her what had happened.

"Please stop at the school," I concluded. "I need Tom to go with us."

"Okay," she agreed. "I'll go on to the landing and see if we can get the plane up here." She looked to the tops of the tall pines and said quietly to herself, "The wind is coming up. I hope the plane can fly."

As I got out of the car at the school with Amy, Tom dashed out of the schoolhouse.

"Amy needs to go to the hospital," I said quietly, trying to be strong because as Tom looked at Amy, horror spread across his face. While he looked, Amy began to jerk and twitch again, her tongue rolling around in her mouth, saliva running out the side of her mouth.

A flat and empty voice came from Tom as he said, "Let's go." He started toward our car but stopped. "What can we do with the schoolkids?"

We stood there a moment, trying to think. Finally we decided that we could take the downvalley kids, the ones who lived on the way to the landing, with us and drop them off at their homes. But what about the ones who lived upvalley?

As we stood there, another car came into view. It was the older brother of some of the upvalley children. Tom ran to the road and stopped him. He willingly agreed to take the upvalley kids with him.

I got in the front seat of our car, holding Amy on my lap. The rest of the children squeezed into the back seat, and we started to the landing. Fearful silence filled the car as we dropped children at various paths and driveways. Amy was lying still in my lap, and her eyes were open, but she didn't seem to be seeing anything. Saliva was running from the side of her mouth. Just as we reached the lakeside, about a mile from where the boat docked, Amy had a violent seizure. As I felt a wetness growing on my lap, she slumped limply in my arms. Stark, cold fear seized me. I thought my child was dying. I began praying the Lord's Prayer aloud. Tom and Sally joined in. The poor child who had been swinging the bat sat shaking in the back seat.

I looked down at Amy through my tears, and I saw she was praying, too. We had taught her the Lord's Prayer as soon as she could talk, and now the words came in jerks as her body continued to convulse. Bubbles oozed out of her mouth, but the words of the Lord's Prayer were clear.

"Thy kingdom come. Thy will be done, on earth as it is in heaven." As I watched her and listened to her pray those words, peace flooded through me. I knew that our Lord was with us and would keep His promise of deliverance to us. In humble gratitude I prayed, "Lord, thank You for giving me this child. She was Yours, and You gave her to me. Now I am giving her back to You. Let Your will be done. For me, I want her just like she was before, beautiful and lively, eating bugs and falling into the flour bin, hugging me when I give her a cookie. I want her just like this never happened. I know You love her far more than I ever could. I know You want only good for her. So Lord, let Your will be done."

All my fear and panic were gone. I knew that Amy was in God's hands. Whether she lived or died, she was in His hands.

We arrived at the landing to find a gale blowing. The winds were gusting to fifty miles per hour. Tom ran to get word from the pilot. I stayed in the car with Amy, and someone came to me, saying that Ernie had refused to fly just a few minutes ago.

"He has to come," I said with quiet desperation.

Then I realized that the *Lady of the Lake* was still at the dock. It should have been gone at least half an hour ago. Mrs. Byrd came to the car and said, "There's a doctor on the boat. He stayed at the lodge last night."

I could scarcely believe it, but the boat had been delayed, and there was a doctor on it.

"Would you see if he will come look at Amy?" I asked her.

She ran toward the boat, and I got out of the car, carrying Amy toward the dock. The wind was blowing so hard I could hardly stand up and carry Amy, too.

Tom met me and took Amy from my sagging arms, cradling her in his strong arms.

"Ernie's going to try to make it, but he's not sure he can with the wind like it is," Tom shouted to me above the wind. Amy was unconscious now, and the bleeding continued.

"Let's get her out of the wind," Tom shouted.

"Here, put her in the back of my station wagon," someone offered.

As we put her down on the back seat, the doctor arrived from the boat. He bent over Amy a moment, then backed out of the car and said, "I'll be right back."

I thought he was going after his little black bag, but in a moment he returned with another man.

"This is Dr. Dwiggens," the first doctor said. "He is a colleague of mine at Stanford Medical Clinic in Palo Alto, California. I didn't know he was in Stehekin until I met him just a few minutes ago on the boat. He is just the doctor you need. He's a respiratory specialist."

I thought, "A respiratory specialist? Why do we need that?" But during the next long half hour I found out. While we waited for the plane, Amy had one seizure after another. Each one was more severe than the last. With each one she bled more, and her breathing stopped for a longer period of time. But here, on this remote end of a lake, way back in the woods, four and one-half hours from the nearest small town, we had a respiratory specialist to keep Amy breathing. Not just a doctor, but the very specialist we needed.

The captain of the *Lady of the Lake* said he would not leave the dock until we were sure the plane could make it. Boat passengers with frightened faces huddled in little groups. Valley people stood here and there, some talking quietly, others crying openly, and still others sitting on the steps with heads bowed, praying.

I was worried about Sally. I didn't think she should go on watching this. I saw Rhoda, Karl's mother, again. I knew that Rhoda would take good care of Sally, so I jumped out of the car and ran to her.

"Will you take care of Sally till we get back?"

"I'd be glad to."

"If she needs any clothes or anything, just go in the house and get them."

I turned to Sally. My heart went out to her tearful little face. I bent down and took hold of her shoulders.

"Honey, we have to take Amy downlake to the doctor. You can stay with Rhoda and Karl until we get back."

She began to cry.

I held her close. "It will be all right, Sally. Amy will be okay, and you'll be fine with Rhoda. I'm sorry, Sweetie, but you really can't go with us. I love you so much. Please don't cry," I said as I brushed the tears away.

I waved to her as she drove away, my heart breaking for the second time that afternoon.

I got back into the station wagon and leaned over the back of the front seat. I talked to the still, gray, unconscious figure. She lay with her head in Tom's lap. His big hand held her head protectively. Her blood was smeared all over his shirt. Tears rolled down his cheeks. His eyes were filled with anguish and tenderness. I knew he would have been willing to give himself to spare this child's pain. I tried to convey my peace to him, and as I talked, my words of encouragement were for him as well as for Amy. She was unconscious and probably couldn't hear me, but if she could, I wanted her to hear that she was okay because Jesus was taking care of her.

Dr. Dwiggens stayed with us, watching closely as Amy's breathing stopped during the seizures. As I watched the still little chest, I stopped breathing, too. From deep inside me came the whispered cry, "Breathe, Amy, breathe." I saw Dr. Dwiggens check his wristwatch again. Still she didn't breathe. We waited. "Doctor!" I gasped.

"She's okay," he assured me. "She's all right," he repeated. And then she breathed. Between seizures the doctor changed her bandages as the blood continued to gush from the wound.

Suddenly Amy opened her eyes and began to cry loudly. The wind carried her cries out to the little crowds of people. I jumped out of the car and shouted to the boat captain, "Thank God! She's crying!"

Murmurs of "Thank God" passed from one group to another. And then we heard it! The sound of a plane engine! Here came the plane swooping over the turmoil of the lake. My eyes filled with tears of joy and gratitude. Ernie had come; he'd made it!

Several of the valley men helped to hold the plane steady in the waves as Tom and I and the two doctors made our way down the heaving dock to the plane.

Ernie looked at us, quickly sizing up the weight.

"You can't all go," he shouted above the wind. "The less weight we have, the better chance we have of making it."

His words grabbed my hopeful heart, and I realized the dangerous situation was not over. Somebody would have to stay behind. I looked at Tom and knew that he would not be able to survive the four and one-half hour boat trip. He needed to go with Amy. Next I looked at the doctors. I wanted them to go. Amy would need them. That left me.

An immense longing to be with my child filled me. How could I stay on this heaving dock and see her fly away in this plane? But if I stayed here, she would have a better chance of making it to the hospital.

"Ernie," I shouted. I clung to his arm and said, "I'll stay, Ernie. If it will help get her out, I'll stay."

Ernie's blue eyes softened, and a hint of mistiness came to them. He put his arm around me and pulled me close to him.

"Your weight won't hurt. You don't weigh anything. Get in." He turned to the doctors. "Which one of you is most necessary?" he shouted. "I can only take one of you. The other will have to stay."

It was decided Dr. Dwiggens should go, and he climbed into the back seat beside me. Amy was handed to him. Tom was in the front seat next to Ernie.

We had a perilous flight. The small plane bounced and tossed around between the mountains. I looked out the little window of the plane and down at the lake and fought with my feelings of fear and joy.

I watched Amy sleeping quietly in Dr. Dwiggens's arms. The roar of the plane and wind was deafening, but I could hear Tom blow his nose from time to time. I reached forward and put my hand on his shoulder. He took my hand in his and held it for a while.

Dr. Dwiggens lightly rested his hand on Amy's chest. From time to time he put his hand to her nose to feel the breath.

Again I looked out the small window. Even from that height I could see great waves tossing on the lake. I remembered the story in the Gospels about Jesus and the Disciples on the storm-tossed lake. The Disciples became frightened and woke the sleeping Jesus. "Teacher, do you not care if we perish?" they asked Him. And Jesus said to them, "Why are you afraid? Have you no faith?" (Mark 4:38, 40 RSV). Then He rose and rebuked the winds and the sea; and there was great calm.

As I looked down at this boiling sea, it did not seem to hear Jesus' rebuke. But my storm-tossed soul did, and once again calmness and peace enveloped me.

17

The plane shuddered as we hopped over the lake. Each time the plane bounced, I was sure it would split apart. When we settled on the water at last, the high waves tossed us about like a cork. I began to get seasick. Amy woke up and started screaming that she was going to be sick. Ernie skillfully guided the plane to the dock, where his son anchored the plane after some great difficulty in the wind. An ambulance waited for us, and soon we were on the way to the hospital. X rays at the Chelan Hospital showed that Amy had a depressed skull fracture. Numerous bone fragments were pressed into her brain. Surgery was the only procedure for lifting the bone and releasing the pressure that was causing the paralysis and seizures. Chelan Hospital was not equipped for such procedures. We would need to transfer Amy to the Wenatchee Hospital. Arrangements were quickly made, a neurosurgeon was alerted that we were on our way, and once more we were in the ambulance. I rode with Amy while Tom followed in our truck, which we had some time ago sent out of Stehekin on the barge. Dr. Dwiggens did not accompany us to Wenatchee but gave all his information to the doctors by phone. The bleeding seemed to be under control, and the seizures were less severe as we raced toward the Wenatchee Hospital.

I had lost all sense of time. I seemed only to be living each moment as it came. I did not look forward or backward. The present moment was the only reality I knew. I was quiet and at peace with each moment.

Amy lay quietly in the ambulance. She drifted in and out of

consciousness. She breathed steadily, and her color was not so gray as before.

As we drove, I looked out the window of the ambulance. The hills were bare and drab after we left the blueness of the lake. Intermittently the brown hills were covered with lush orchards whose trees were heavy with nearly ripe apples. Large wooden boxes stood in tall stacks, waiting to be filled with the fruit.

My heart warmed as the realization came to me. Even these brown hills, which seem barren, can produce luscious fruit under the proper circumstances. Looking at the bare hills, one would not think it possible, yet those huge wooden boxes would be full, and beautiful red apples would be sent throughout the country to feed hundreds of thousands of people.

I looked at Amy and the present situation. It, too, looked pretty barren. Could it be possible that even this barrenness could produce fruit? It was hard to believe as I looked at her still little figure lying on the stretcher. Her left hand was drawn into a tight fist and held rigidly to the bloody shirt. The bloody bandage dominated her head, making her look very tiny and helpless indeed.

The driver radioed to the hospital, telling them we would be there in five minutes. As we came to the edge of the city, he turned on the siren, and we moved unobstructed through the traffic. As we backed up to the emergency room door, two nurses and a doctor rushed out. I was asked to sign a permission paper, and then I found myself standing alone in the hallway. Tom arrived shortly, and we stood there with our arms around each other, literally holding each other up. A nurse came out and directed us to the chapel where we could wait for the doctor to finish examining Amy.

We stepped into the solitude of the chapel, and immediately I felt strengthened. God was surely here in this hospital, too, and He would certainly look after His precious child. Once more I reminded the Lord (and myself) that I had given Amy to Him, that she was totally in His gracious hands to do with as He wished. One look at Tom showed me he had not experienced this release. He sat humped over in the chair, his face in his hands, quiet sobs shaking his body.

"Lord," I asked, "how do I comfort my husband? His heart is breaking. What can I do for him?"

"Love him," was the reply. "You can love him, but he must come to Me for comfort."

I sat close to Tom and rubbed his heaving back. "She's okay, Tom. She's in the Lord's hands. He'll take care of her."

The sobbing began to subside. He straightened up and blew his nose. At that moment a small man in plaid slacks and long-sleeved blue shirt came into the chapel.

"Are you Mr. and Mrs. Olson?" he asked.

"Yes," Tom answered.

"Hello, I am Dr. Meade." He extended his hand to Tom. "I'm a neurosurgeon. I have just examined Amy." His voice was quiet and reassuring. He gave us confidence as he spoke. He talked quickly, explaining what he had found and what he would have to do to correct it. He spoke of the chances that he might have to take, of possible problems he would run into, and the risks involved. With our consent he would begin immediately. The operating room was ready; it had been prepared while we were en route. As he left, he directed us to where we could sign the necessary consent papers. As we stepped into the hallway, we saw a stretcher coming quickly up the hall. On it lay a tiny figure covered with a white sheet. A fresh bandage covered most of the head. I was shocked to realize it was Amy. The orderly and nurse stopped the stretcher beside us. The nurse spoke loudly to Amy, "Amy, here's your mama and daddy. Wake up and say hello to them."

Tiny brown eyes opened and looked at us. As she recognized us, there was movement under the sheet as she tried to reach out to us. The right hand reached up, and the right knee came up, but the left side of her body lay lifeless.

I bent down to her and kissed her. "You have a nice ride with the nurse. She'll take good care of you. Daddy and I will be right here." As I kissed her again, my face became wet from her tears.

Tom kissed her and squeezed her hand. His eyes said to her what he could not trust his voice to say.

After we had signed the papers, we went back to the chapel. I

sat down, but Tom could not. He paced back and forth. Finally
he nearly exploded with, "If I'd only been out there, this never
would have happened."

"Tom, don't do that to yourself. Even if you'd been there, you
couldn't have stopped it. You know how fast children run. You
couldn't have stopped her if you'd been standing right beside her.
It's not your fault, Tom. It's an accident. It's just like I told the
boy and his mother; it's an accident. It's nobody's fault. Please,
Tom, don't blame yourself."

He sat down with his head in his hands. We were quiet for a
few minutes.

"Tom," I said softly, "it's not your fault, and blaming yourself
won't help Amy one bit right now. But if you pray for her, you
can help her."

He shook his head steadily, and an agonizing groan escaped his
throat.

"Tom, look up there on the wall. See that sign. Come on. Look
up there, and read it."

Slowly he raised his face from his hands. My heart reached out
to him as I saw the agony on his tear-streaked face. He blinked
the tears from his eyes and began to read in a quiet, husky voice,
"Ask, and it will be given you; seek and you will find; knock, and
it will be opened to you. For every one who asks receives; and he
who seeks finds, and to him who knocks it will be opened." (Matt.
7:7-8 RSV).

"Ask Him, Tom. You know He'll answer."

Tom bowed his head and spoke silently to the Lord. I do not
know what he said, but I saw what the Lord did for him. He
stopped shaking and became calmer. He sat quietly for some time.
Finally he took my hand and smiled at me. Still he did not speak.
We sat in silence together, waiting and knowing it would be a
long wait. There was nothing to do but wait.

18

Two and a half hours later, Dr. Meade returned to the chapel.

"Amy is doing fine," he said. "She's in the recovery room now and will go from there in a couple of hours to intensive care. You will be able to see her a few minutes there."

It sounded good, but we wanted to know more. Dr. Meade was very open and always answered all our questions. We greatly appreciated his openness. He told us Amy's skull had been shattered into five pieces at the point of impact. He had retrieved these pieces, one of which was depressed an inch. He had cleaned the wound site and had been amazed at how uncontaminated the area was. He had found no internal bleeding. All the blood had gone out of the head, and there was none between the brain and the skull. Miraculously the dura, the parchmentlike covering over the brain, had not been punctured. This was exceedingly important in the prevention of infection. Dr. Meade also reported incredulously that there was no bruise on the brain and only an unbelievably small amount of swelling. He said he had reshaped the bone fragments, wired them together, and wired them back in place. All Amy's vital signs were stable, but she would be watched very carefully, especially for signs of more seizures. He said it was very probable that she would continue to have seizures, possibly all her life. Time would tell.

We gratefully shook Dr. Meade's hand, thanking him for his interest and skill. The tears in my eyes reinforced my words of praise, and Dr. Meade smiled an especially warm smile and patted my shoulder. I could tell he, too, was pleased with the outcome.

Had he known that God was at his elbow the entire time? I knew He had been there, and the results confirmed it.

Tom and I wept with joy and thanked the Lord for His mercy. Then we went to the phone and called our parents, Tom's in California and mine in Florida. We also called Ernie so that he could relay the information to Sally and the people in Stehekin.

For another two hours we waited. Finally a nurse came to us and led us to the intensive care area. As we walked, I tried to prepare Tom for what he would see. Having had surgery seven times myself and having spent many months in the hospital, I knew what we would probably see. I told Tom that there would probably be IV's and plasma hooked up to Amy. She would probably be very pale and, of course, have a huge bandage on her head. It was even possible that she would not respond to us. Tom received my words with no comment. He simply nodded his head.

The nurse pushed open the door, and we went into a room large enough to hold four beds. That smell peculiar to hospitals filled my nostrils. The light was subdued except where a nurse was working. The steady beep of a heart monitor underscored the groans of a woman with both legs in traction in the first bed.

"Amy's over here," the nurse said kindly, and led us behind the white curtain.

I stepped up beside the bed and looked at my baby. She was sleeping as peacefully as she had been the first time I saw her cuddled in a basket. She was not quite so pink this time, but she certainly was not pale. Instead of the pink bow taped to her abundant black hair, there was a large white gauze turban. Yet I distinctly felt she was once more being given to me. God was giving her back to me to love and enjoy, yet she was, in fact, His. I reached out and took the still, small hand in mine.

I turned to Tom, who was standing beside me. There were tears in his eyes again, but these were tears of joy mixed with the pain. A prayer of thanksgiving burst from his lips, and he began speaking to God outloud, "Thank You, Father. Thank You for saving this precious child. Thank You, Father."

Hearing Tom's voice, Amy opened her eyes. She watched Tom as he prayed. When he stopped, she started the prayer that we always said before she and Sally went to bed. Tom and I joined her tiny, confident voice.

"Dear God, please hear our evening prayer. Thank You for Your love and care. Thank You for this happy day"—my voice cracked at this point—"for home and friends, and work and play. Bless the ones we love tonight, and keep us all till morning light."

Tom and I said, "Amen," but Amy continued.

"And Jesus, please help Helen to feel better. Help her to use her arm and leg again. Thank You, Jesus. Amen."

I looked at the nurse, who was standing at the end of the bed. Her chin was trembling. "Helen is a neighbor we had in Ohio. She had a stroke a few weeks ago and is paralyzed on one side," I explained.

"What a beautiful thing for this little child to be praying for an old woman at this moment," the nurse said as she blinked the tears away. I heard a nose being blown across the room. I looked up and saw a middle-aged woman standing beside the bed of an old man hooked to another heart monitor.

I looked back at Amy. "You are a beautiful child, Amy, and Daddy and I love you." I kissed the tiny, soft cheek. She tried to reach for me, but the board that kept one arm straight for the IV prevented her. She started to cry and asked to sit in my lap.

"Oh I'd love to hold you, but it wouldn't really be very comfortable for you, Amy. You'll feel much better lying down. I'll just sit here beside you and hold your hand."

The nurse found another chair for Tom, and we both sat as close to Amy as possible. She drifted back to sleep, and a quietness settled over our part of the room. I began to think of all the hours my mother had sat beside my bed. I wondered how she had felt through all those vigils. A new love and appreciation and understanding for my mother filled my heart. Now I understood the mixture of pain and joy that I'd seen in her eyes so often.

Tom and I traded chairs, as he wanted to hold Amy's hand awhile. Amy was awakened by the change. When she saw Tom sitting closest to her, she smiled faintly and reached her left arm and hand through the bars on the bed.

"If you'll come a little closer, Daddy, I'll scratch your back," she offered, knowing how much her daddy liked his back scratched.

"Thank you, Amy," Tom said in a very trembling voice, "but you can do it later. Just rest now."

"Okay, Daddy," she agreed, and drifted back to sleep.

"She can use her left arm!" Tom whispered joyfully.

The rest of the night became a blur in my mind. We sat with Amy and watched for any indication of a recurring seizure. We walked up and down the hallway, alone sometimes and together at other times. One nurse asked us whether we had eaten any dinner. We remembered that we had not. A few minutes later the nurse asked us to come into the room next to the intensive care unit. There, sitting on the bedside table of the unused hospital room, was a tray with sandwiches and salads and coffee.

"I thought you might be hungry," she said. "Eat what you can. And there's a telephone over there. Please feel free to use it."

Again and again for the next twelve hours we were impressed by the thoughtfulness of the nurses and doctors and staff members of that hospital.

Twice that night the phone rang in the ICU. We heard the nurse reporting briefly on Amy's condition. One call, she told us, was from the doctor who had taken care of Amy at the boat. The second caller was Tom's father, a retired physician. After talking with him, the nurse transferred the call to the adjoining room, where Tom and I talked with Poppie. He said he had been so shocked when we first called him that he had not thought clearly about what we'd said. Now he was full of questions about the procedures and her condition. He offered to come up from California if he could be of any comfort to us. He also offered money to help with the costs. What loving and caring parents Tom and I were both blessed with!

By early the next morning, Amy's IV and blood bottles had been changed several times. There had been no recurrence of seizures, and she was weakly using her left arm and leg. Blood pressure and pulse were good. So Tom and I left to find someplace to sleep for a few hours.

When we returned about one o'clock, Amy was being prepared

to move to the pediatrics ward. With great joy we followed her crib up the elevator and into the children's area. She was placed in the last room near the nurses station; it had a large window overlooking the town and the hills and orchards. There was another little girl in the room. She, too, was suffering from a head injury sustained in an automobile accident. She had had extensive surgery and because of the injury had lost many bodily functions. She was also unable to speak, or at least she did not respond when spoken to. Part of me cried out in pain for her, and the other part of me rejoiced that God had chosen to give Amy back to us whole. Amy continued to improve rapidly. She never seemed to experience any pain. Only once did she say anything to me about her head hurting, and that was the first night in ICU. She was plenty irritable at times for the next few days but never expressed having pain. I was sure this was God's protection for her, and I thanked Him for it.

As I sat with Amy through the next days, I was continually amazed at the goodness of God's people. For example, I heard the phone ring at the nurses station. Presently a nurse came to me and said the phone call was for me.

"Is it long distance?" I asked as I followed her.

"No. It's a local call."

"Wonder who it is? I don't know anyone in Wenatchee," I said.

The caller was a woman who had been on the boat in Stehekin the day the accident happened. She wanted me to know that she had been praying for Amy, and she wondered how Amy was doing. This incident was repeated time and again. Finally the nurse would come and say, "I know you don't know anyone in Wenatchee, but the phone is for you."

When we left Stehekin that day on the plane, I had not taken a purse. In fact, I had not taken my purse out of the house. Tom rarely carried money because there really was no need for it. There was little use for money except when we went downlake to town. This particular day, however, Tom had seven dollars in his wallet. That was all the money we had. The checkbook was also at home. Yet somehow we never lacked for anything. We had stayed in a private home that first morning with a relative of the woman who was with her father in ICU. We had eaten in the hospital cafeteria, and the food was inexpensive. A friend who had been in Wenatchee when Amy's accident occurred came to see us and gave us ten dollars. I felt that was ample for my meals when Tom would leave to go back to Stehekin to be with Sally and open the school again. We had found a sleeping room in a retired nurse's home two blocks from the hospital. She did not want to be paid until we left at the end of Amy's stay in the hospital. So I felt very secure as far as money was concerned.

One afternoon Tom left to go to the library to get some books. Amy wanted me to read to her, and I was interested in reading something myself while she slept. While Tom was gone, a woman from a nearby town came to visit us. She was a frequent visitor to Stehekin and had been in our home several times for the Bible study. Because of a health problem, Mrs. Strong, who was a widow, was not able to drive. Her friend had brought her to Wenatchee to see us. I was delighted to see Mrs. Strong. We had a nice visit, and Amy loved the little gifts she brought. When Mrs. Strong was ready to leave, she asked me if I needed anything. I assured her I was being very well taken care of.

"Can I give you any money?" she asked.

"No, we're doing just fine. Bill gave me ten dollars the other night, and that is ample."

"What about your room? Can I pay that for you?"

"That's very kind of you, but no. It really won't be very much, and I'll pay it when we leave."

"How much will it be?" she pressed.

I told her, and she got out her checkbook. "Let me pay it for you. I want to do that for you and Tom," she said as she began to write the check.

I had never been able to accept money from people. It was hard for me to receive any favor, especially when I felt I didn't need it. But I could see that it meant a lot to Mrs. Strong to be able to give us something. Against my own feelings, I accepted the check, being very sure that I did not need it, and that I was taking it only to please her.

"Thank you," I said.

Immediately she took it back. "That check is no good to you. You need cash. Let me go cash it for you," she said and disappeared out the door.

Half an hour later, she returned. "I couldn't get it cashed. It was made out to you. The hospital wouldn't accept it. Neither would any place else I went. Besides that, it was my last check, so I can't write another. My friend and I have emptied our pockets, and we have come up with thirteen dollars. I'm sorry that's all we have between us. But do take it."

It was very hard for me to take the money, especially now that I knew it was all they had. But Mrs. Strong was so earnest I had to accept it. I thanked her, and she hugged me and left.

Fifteen minutes later Dr. Meade came in to check on Amy. I was surprised to see him because he had already been in once that day and it was only early afternoon. He examined Amy again and rechecked the wound. Then he said, "I think if we had a helmet to protect Amy's head, we could start letting her get up a few minutes at a time."

At that instant Tom came back into the room, and he and Dr. Meade discussed the type of helmet that would be best. He suggested that Tom go to the sporting goods stores and see what he could find.

After Dr. Meade left, Tom turned to me. "Well, that's good news, but how will we pay for a helmet?"

I grinned and pulled the thirteen dollars from my pocket. "How about this money?"

"Where'd you get that?" he asked.

I explained how it just happened to be in my pocket.

"Terrific! How much is it?"

"Thirteen dollars."

"Thirteen? That's not enough to buy a helmet. They cost twice that."

"Maybe so, but that's what God just gave us."

Tom took it and kissed Amy and me and headed for the sporting goods stores. There were three in town, but he headed first to the one Dr. Meade had suggested. Tom explained to the owner and clerk what he needed. There was one helmet in stock. It was Amy's size and easily adaptable for our needs.

Tom was delighted, but he still had to ask the question, "How much is it?"

"Well, it's $25.95, but since you'll be using it for your daughter's protection from this terrible injury, I'll give you a discount. Let's see"—he mumbled to himself as he figured the cost—"that'll be thirteen dollars exactly."

No doubt the man wondered why Tom stood there staring at him awhile before he dug exactly thirteen dollars out of his pocket.

That night Dr. Meade and Tom worked on the helmet, adapting it to Amy's needs. And I began my trips up and down the hall pulling a Radio Flyer wagon with an inquisitive and sometimes demanding passenger. It seemed I walked forty miles during the next ten days.

One morning after Tom had gone back to Stehekin to be with Sally and to teach, I was watching Amy as she played at the little table in her room. As she got up to do something else, she staggered. I dismissed the action, thinking perhaps the helmet caused her balance problems. But the staggering increased over the next few hours. While Amy was sleeping that afternoon, I mentioned the problem to the nurse. She wrote it down and said she would bring it to the doctor's attention. Later that afternoon the pediatrician who had also been seeing Amy came to check on her. I told him what I had observed. He got Amy out of bed and asked her to walk for him. They were good friends now, but they had started out on rocky ground as far as Amy was concerned. The first time Dr. Newman came to see her, she told him to go away. "I don't want you to bother me," she had said. He was very amused by this and very quickly wooed her into his camp.

This afternoon she was eager to perform for him, and as she walked back and forth at his direction, she staggered even worse than she had that morning. My heart sank. I knew her injury had been over the motor strip and even though she had had full but weakened use of the previously paralyzed side since the surgery, I was concerned that there was damage. Dr. Newman watched a

few minutes, then reached out and pulled Amy onto his lap.
With genuine relief he said, "You're okay, kid. It's just the medication. Sometimes Dilantin does this. After a couple days off the
medicine you'll be fine."

He was right. Amy's medication was reduced to only phenobarbital to prevent seizures.

"Thank You, Lord," I rejoiced. "Thank You that it was not evidence of damage."

Tom and Sally came to Wenatchee for the weekend. I was so
relieved to see Sally. I had been concerned about her being separated from us during this hard time, but we also knew it would
have been very hard for her to be with us. She seemed glad to see
that Amy was not really too different from her usually active self.

Early the next week Amy seemed rather listless one morning.
She didn't want to ride in the wagon. I would have been delighted
except that I wondered why she would pass up a ride. I took her
on my lap and started to read to her. After a couple of pages she
leaned her forehead on my cheek, and I felt as though fire had
touched me. I put my hand to her head and felt the highest fever
I've ever experienced. I quickly put Amy in bed and went after
the nurse.

The nurse took Amy's temperature and immediately grabbed
her out of bed and ran to the bathtub room. Amid Amy's screams
we dunked her in cool water. Medication was brought to her, and
we continued to bathe her. Shortly after we got her back in bed,
Dr. Meade arrived. There was little else he could do, but I was
grateful for his being there.

"What's causing the fever, doctor?" I asked.

"I don't know," he said honestly. "It could be that infection
has set in. But it usually happens much sooner than this if it's
going to happen at all. There'll be some people up here in a few
minutes from the lab to do a culture."

He left shortly, and five minutes later I was surprised to see him
coming in again, this time accompanied by Dr. Newman. Dr.
Meade was carrying a sterile package of some sort. He took Amy
out of bed and sat her on my lap. He took off the bandage, and
the two men conferred about the wound.

"Looks okay to me," said Dr. Newman.

The package was opened, and instruments for doing the culture were exposed. A sterile swab was put into the open hole in Amy's head, and the material on it was transferred to the culture dish. This was done several times. Dr. Newman finished preparing the test materials while Dr. Meade redressed the wound.

"It will be twenty-four hours before we'll have the results," he told me.

I knew that it would be as long a wait for him as it would be for me. What a wonderful man he was, besides being such a competent doctor.

That night both doctors came back to see Amy. Dr. Meade was obviously worried. "I sure hate to open that up again," he said to his colleague, "but if there's infection in there, that bone has to come out and the sooner the better."

"But it looks good," Dr. Newman replied. "I don't think that's the source of the problem. Kids will spike a temp like this over nothing. Maybe she's picked up something. Let's wait. It would be too bad to open it up if we really didn't need to."

As I watched the men conferring and understood their deep concern for my child, I prayed that the Lord would guide them. "Tell them, Jesus. Tell Dr. Meade what he should do."

Dr. Meade stood silently, looking at Amy. His hands were pushed deep into his pockets. He frowned as he concentrated. At last he moved, took his hands out of his pockets, and sighed deeply.

"Okay, we'll wait for the culture."

The next morning he was back again. He reported to me that during the night Amy's temperature had stayed reasonably low as long as the medication was in effect. Without that, it started to climb.

Twenty-four hours and twenty minutes after the test was taken, the two doctors were back in Amy's room. Dr. Newman beamed. "The culture is clear," he announced.

"The usual harmless stuff wasn't even there. It was perfectly clear," said Dr. Meade with a puzzled look.

I smiled and thanked God for His sterilization of Amy's wound.

We never determined why Amy had that high fever. It went away in another day. There were no other symptoms of any problem.

I was delighted a few days later when Dr. Meade told us we could go home. I called Ernie to tell him not to bring Tom and Sally out but to plan on taking Amy and me back. At the appointed time a friend came to drive us from Wenatchee to Chelan. It was a very different feeling I experienced as we rode back between the hills and along the Columbia River to the lake and to the dock where the plane waited. I not only felt different. I was different. God had shown me clearly that He is in charge of all things and that He can and will provide for all our needs in ways that are predictable and in ways that are totally unpredictable. I praised Him for His love and for the people through whom He worked: Dr. Dwiggens, Ernie, the nurses, Dr. Meade and Dr. Newman, and others. Praise You, God, for all these people.

19

"I need to stop at the drugstore to get the prescription filled," I said to the friend who was driving Amy and me from Wenatchee to the plane in Chelan. "I'd also like to call my mother and tell her that we are taking Amy home."

While the pharmacist was getting the phenobarbital for Amy, I talked with my mother in Florida.

"Hello, Mother. I just wanted to let you know that we are taking Amy home now. Yes, she's doing fine. No, there have been no seizures, but she will be taking phenobarb daily to prevent any recurrence of the seizures. Yes, I hate to see her have to take it, too, but that's sure better than her having more seizures. Yes, I asked Dr. Meade about the possibility of her becoming addicted to it. He said it was a very slim chance that anyone taking the drug for this reason would become addicted to it. As a matter of fact most people even forget to take it. He felt it is the people who are taking it for reasons other than seizure prevention that become addicted because they want the drug. So I'm not going to be concerned about it. Amy is in the Lord's hands. He'll take care of her.

"And Mother, there is one more thing I want to tell you." I took a deep breath, feeling a lump of emotion coming into my throat. "Mother, I just wanted you to know that I think you are the most beautiful mother in the world. I never really understood what you went through all those years with me and my problems with polio, the paralysis, the surgeries, the time I was so near death, and even just the constant care and therapy you and Daddy gave me. I never understood it till I sat there beside my own child, praying for her life to be restored. Now I know, Mother. And I think you are beautiful. I love you. Thank you for loving me." I finished with my voice trembling and tears dropping on the phone. Proverbs 31:28 came to my mind: "Her children arise up, and call her blessed." Praise God! I have one of the most blessed mothers in the world.

I blew my nose and put away my handkerchief, paid the smiling pharmacist, and went back to the car. My friend took us to the plane and waved to us as we climbed aboard.

It was a glorious day to fly. Totally the opposite of the last day that we had flown in this plane with Ernie. The sky was clear and bluer than the lake, which is known for its blueness. The sun was warm for a fall day. Amy and I looked down on the tiny orchards filled with busy, ant-sized men picking and carrying apples.

As we passed the occupied area and pressed into the un-populated mountains, a tinge of fear grew around my heart. "You are taking this child back to isolation in the wilderness. You are taking her away from medical help. Don't you think that's rather silly? Aren't you taking a big chance? Have you forgotten so quickly what a terrifying experience you have had?"

I listened to that voice for a few minutes as the tiny plane wound its way between the mountains, carrying us farther and farther away from doctors and hospitals. I was almost to the point of saying, "Turn around. Take us back. I'm afraid to go back there."

Just then Matthew 28:20 popped into my head: "Lo, I am with you alway, even unto the end of the world." I realized the Lord was with us, even to the end of this lake and back into this far part of the world. I knew that He would take care of all our needs. Hadn't He already shown us that? Psalm 33:20-22 says, "Our soul waiteth for the Lord: he is our help and our shield. For our heart shall rejoice in him, because we have trusted in his holy name. Let thy mercy, O Lord, be upon us, according as we hope in thee."

With new joy and hope in Him I ordered the spirit of fear to depart in His name. Once more the day was beautiful and clear, and my heart was filled with delight at returning to Sally and Tom and our little house in the woods.

The plane landed, and we were helped out. By the time Amy and I reached the end of the dock and stepped onto the land, we were enfolded in outstretched arms and cheerful calls. Edith picked Amy up and kissed her. "How are you feeling, Amy?" she asked. She had been out of the valley when the accident happened and had returned only a few days before us to learn of our experience.

"Fine," was Amy's quiet response.

"Can she have an ice-cream cone?" Edith asked me. I nodded, and away they went toward the restaurant.

"Come right back. She needs to get some rest. She's had a big day already," I called to them.

Later that afternoon, while Amy slept, I started to go through the big stack of mail that had accumulated. Tom had opened some of it, but most of it sat waiting for me. I sorted out advertisement mail and then began on the pile of personal mail.

The first few things were letters from people who had heard about our experience, relating their love and hope for us. Then I opened a bill from the anesthesiologist. It was one hundred and forty-five dollars. With a sigh I laid it aside and went on through the stack. Three letters later there was a note from one of the men in the valley. His note read, "I am glad Amy is okay. She's a sweet little girl. I love her." A check for twenty-five dollars was attached. This man lived alone and had somewhat of a gruff manner about him, at least Amy had always thought so. She had, in fact, been afraid of him because he told her once that he was going to put her in a hole. She did not understand that he was teasing her. One night some time after he had told her that, he came to our home for a rare visit. Amy was in bed but not asleep. Her little voice called to me. When I went to her bed, she whispered quietly, "Is that ——— ?" Even in the dim light I could see how big her eyes were.

"Yes, he's visiting with Daddy."

She was quiet a few moments and then jumped out of bed and grabbed her half-empty Easter basket. She tiptoed to the doorway where she could see the color of all the jelly beans. Quickly she dug through them, picking out all the red ones. They were her favorites. "Here Mommy," she said, handing them to me. "Give these to ——— for me."

When I gave them to the man, he sat silently looking at the five jelly beans in his big, calloused hand. Finally he said, barely above a whisper, "Well, I'll be damned."

My heart was warmed as I looked at his note. I gratefully laid his gift on top of the doctor's bill.

I went on with the mail. The next letter was from a family in Ohio. Tom had taught their daughter in the girls' school there. They had been touring the West the past summer and had spent a few fun-filled days with us. Mr. Wilson had taken a great liking to both our girls. He played with them, took them for walks ("hikes," they called them), carried them around on his shoulders, and even picked a three-pound can full of berries for them. His wife and I had many inspiring talks, and I appreciated her beautiful letter. However, I was shocked to see a money order for us in the amount of one hundred dollars. With trembling hand and grateful heart I laid the check on top of the doctor's bill.

I went through a few school letters and then opened the last letter. It was from another valley resident. His lovely note was also accompanied by a gift of twenty dollars.

Incredible! Minutes before I had opened a bill for one hundred and forty-five dollars wondering how it would get paid. In the same mail stack were three gifts totaling exactly one hundred and forty-five dollars! "Thank You, Lord," I prayed. "I believe; Lord, help my unbelief."

After school we had a glorious family reunion. I was so happy to be with Sally again. I had so missed this quiet, sweet little person. What a joy she has always been to me!

Later in the afternoon Mrs. Bowles's old pickup stopped in front of our house. Out she hopped and shuffled toward the door. She and Herb had lived in Japan for some time, and I often felt the traditional Japanese style of walking had rubbed off on Mrs. Bowles.

Her kind face was glowing with a secret when I opened the door. But she wasn't going to let us in on it until she was good and ready. She talked with Amy and Sally, asking many questions and telling her favorite stories.

Finally she said to Tom and me, "I've brought you something."

She reached into her bag and produced a can with a slit in the top and a card taped to the side.

"The people in the valley wanted to share with you and express our love and concern," she said. "This can has been sitting on the counter in the coffee shop. There will be many nickels and dimes in it because even the children have shared. It will help you with your expenses. God bless you."

We thanked her and hugged her and waved as she drove away. I looked at the card and was moved when I read

> To a dear family, Tom, Lois, Sally, and Amy, With all good wishes from the Stehekin Folks. Friends are very precious; this is a small token in an expression of friendship.

A few days later she returned with a box of money. The total of the two gifts equaled what the bill would be from Ernie. When I gave him the cash, he said, "Oh don't worry about it. There's no hurry. Pay what you can when you can."

I insisted that he take it. "It's a very small way for us to thank you for what you did. And anyway, this is all compliments of the beautiful people in this valley."

The first evening Amy and I were home, we all had a joyful dinner together. Soon it was time for bed. Amy asked me to help her get her nightie on. As I pulled off her dress, I saw tiny red dots covering her chest.

I collapsed onto the chair. "Dear God," I prayed silently. "What now? What is this on her chest? It looks like an allergy rash."

"Tom, look at this," I said limply.

He looked carefully and said in a guarded voice, "Looks like she's allergic to something."

"But what?"

"What has she had that she hasn't had before?"

"Nothing," I said. I sat up straight. "Except phenobarb. She had it in the hospital, but she's never had it before that." I was horrified. "You don't suppose she's allergic to that?"

"I don't know," he answered. "But it could be. She had a reaction to the other medicine."

"But if she can't take this, what will she take? That's all the antiseizure medicine there is."

"We'll have to let the doctor figure that one out. I wouldn't give her any more of the medicine until the doctor sees her. You'd better take her back tomorrow."

All at once I burst into tears. It seemed my emotional rope had snapped. I'd thought I had everything under control. I'd thought everything was over, and now here was something else. I wasn't at all sure I could handle something else. What should I do? If I gave her the medicine and she was really allergic to it, she could get into real trouble. If I didn't give it to her, maybe she would have another seizure. What should I do?

"Come on now," Tom said, pulling me up into his arms. "This is a small thing compared to what we've been through. And remember, we gave it all over to the Lord, didn't we?"

I nodded and sniffed.

"Okay then. It's His affair."

"Yes, but what should I do?"

"Give her one more dose tonight. One more teaspoon won't hurt, since she's not showing a gross reaction. And that will buy us more time for the seizure prevention. Then tomorrow you can take her out first thing."

I did as he said, praying all the while that it was the right thing to do. I put her to bed and then slept beside her so I could hear if she had any problems.

The next day Dr. Meade was surprised to see us. When I showed him her chest, which looked the same as it had the night before, he was astounded. He asked the nurse to get Dr. Newman. Minutes later the two men were once more conferring over Amy.

"You're right. It is an allergic reaction. But I can't believe it," said Dr. Newman. "Nobody's allergic to phenobarb!"

"Well Amy is," said Dr. Meade. He shook his head in disbelief.

"What now?" I asked. "What kind of medicine should she

have? You said she would need to take this medicine for a year. What will we do now?"

Dr. Meade sighed. "There isn't anything else to give her. We'll just have to take her off all medication and hope there's no problem. She certainly can't take this or Dilantin. But as long as you're here," he said, changing the subject, "let me show you how I want you to clean the wound and dress it. In about a week I want you to begin doing this." And he proceeded to show me how to take care of the wound. "You won't need to come back for three to four weeks unless there is some problem."

A few minutes later I sat in the truck. "Lord, is this Your work again? Are You behind her inability to tolerate these two medicines?"

A strong *yes* filled my mind, and I knew it was the Lord speaking to me: "I have healed her. She doesn't need this medicine."

I bowed my head humbly, and let the tears of relief and thanksgiving flow. "Oh how great is thy goodness, which thou hast laid up for them that fear thee. . . . Blessed be the Lord: for he hath shewed me his marvellous kindness" (Ps. 31:19, 21).

20

The boat wound its way slowly up the lake. The trees on the slopes of the mountains shouted the season with their radiant leaves of gold, red, purple, and orange. The summer days when the boat was crowded with passengers were past, and now the boat was only sparsely populated. There were a few hardy tourists, but for the most part there were men whose red hats and jackets told why they were heading into the mountains. One of those men walked amiably along the aisle of the boat. The wrinkles on his face betrayed his age, as did the gray hair that managed to be seen under the red plaid hunter's hat. Yet the warm smile, the sparkle in his eyes, and a lightness about his step, affirmed that this man was filled with life. As he made his way down the aisle of the boat, he noticed a pleasant-looking man in his thirties sitting near a window, quietly reading a picture book to his child. It was an ordinary-enough scene except that the child was wearing a hockey helmet.

The older man sat down in the seat in front of the father and child and turned around to listen to the story. His frequent chuckles showed that he was enjoying the story as much as the child. When the story was over, a friendly conversation began that marked the beginning of a relationship that would have life-changing consequences. It was indeed a divine encounter.

"Where are you two headed?" the older man asked.

"Home," replied the little girl.

"Home? Do you live in Stehekin?"

"Yep!"

He was looking intently at the child now. It was evident that she was not wearing the helmet just for fun. One could see that under the helmet on the right side there was no hair. A certain paleness in the child's face revealed she had been through some great trauma in the recent past.

A flash of memory passed through the older man.

"Oh! I bet you're the little girl that got hurt at the school in Stehekin," he said with a knowing look.

"How did you know?" asked the child, thoroughly puzzled.

"I read it in the newspaper," he confessed. "I live in Manson, which is not far from Chelan, and I take the Chelan paper. Let's see if I can remember your name."

He rolled his eyes and worked his closed lips in an exaggeratedly thoughtful way while he rubbed his chin.

"I know," he nearly shouted, his eyes opening wide. He pointed his finger at the child and said with great excitement, "Amy! That's your name. Amy!"

Amy was very impressed. She looked at her daddy as if to say, "Wow! This man knows who I am, and I've never seen him before."

The man introduced himself as Bruce Groseclose. His statement that he was a retired Methodist minister sent a shock of excitement through Tom.

Tom began to share about Amy's accident and all the Lord had so miraculously done for us all and that he and Amy were returning from an appointment with the doctor. The conversation stretched into sharing that lasted an hour, an hour and a half, two hours, and on and on. Amy long ago had squeezed from between them and helped pilot the boat, talked with other passengers, read stories, talked with her ever-present Teddy, and finally went to sleep on an empty seat with Tom's coat over her.

As Tom and Bruce shared, an exciting idea was allowed to be born. It had been carried around inside Tom's head for some time. As he spoke of it, he found that the Lord had planted the same seed in Bruce's mind and heart.

Tom told of how meaningful the Bible studies had been for many of us in Stehekin. It had provided the basis for great sharing and growth in all of us. Yet we were somehow missing something. We felt we needed to be worshiping together as well as studying together. An idea had begun to take shape in Tom's mind.

"Is there some way that a church could be started in Stehekin?" he asked Bruce. "I know there is no way that such a handful of people could support a minister, yet we do feel the need for a true worship service."

The rest of the boat trip flew past as these men searched out possibilities for making this idea become a reality. There were many things to consider, such as the small number of people interested and the remoteness of the place. Yet there was also the fact that there were many tourists in the summer who would be interested in having services available.

As the boat docked and the men parted company, Bruce promised to work on seeing how this idea could become a reality. It was to take him many hours of work that fall and winter before he wrote us of his exciting news the next spring. But there were more steps of growth in store for Tom and me before that time came.

Tom's experience occurred in late November. As he was taking a hike one Saturday, something happened that planted another seed in his mind and heart. He was not aware of what the seed would grow into, but he knew without a doubt that a seed had been planted. When he shared it with me, I was amazed at how similar it was to my own experience in very nearly the same place. After Tom shared with me, he sat down at the desk in front of the big windows looking into the woods and wrote this account to a friend.

> I have just had one of the most exhilarating experiences of my life, and I want to share it with you before the splendor of it fades (if it ever could). Today was such a beautiful day that I decided to take a walk. I chose the Stehekin River Trail because it is close to our house. There were only a few clouds floating high in the sky. The air was crisp and invigorating. The ground was moist from the recent snow, and the leaves that had fallen on the ground provided me with a very soft carpet to walk on. Part of the old Stehekin Road made up the beginning of the trail, but it gradually faded into a "normal" trail. I crossed empty stream

beds and gazed at huge virgin pines. The trail meandered close to a stream. The water was clear, although the stream was crowded with trees that had fallen during last spring's high water. The trees were piled on one another, creating a dam of sorts. I looked for signs of life beneath the surface of the water, but found none. On the other side of the "dam," the water was teeming with salmon, all of them engaging in their instinctive love play. I watched with fascination as the males chased away other males who tried to cross into their territory. Not wanting to disturb their ritual, I continued along the trail. I was amazed at the many varieties of fungi and mushrooms that were still protruding through the soft, moist earth, even this late in the year.

Suddenly the trail turned away from the river and started to go up a steep slope. I noticed a couple of deer runs branching off from the trail I was walking on. I heard a sound that resembled the cry of a hawk, so I moved rapidly up the slope, hoping to get a glimpse of the bird. I paused when I reached an open plateau, but as I looked down on the Stehekin River, I saw only seagulls flying overhead, eager to clean up the doomed salmon. I watched, hoping to get a glimpse of Jonathan Livingston Seagull. As I watched I began to see in the distance a large bird that was easy for me to identify. It flew gracefully toward the bluff I was standing on. Then it turned and flew parallel to me over the river. The magnificent bald eagle was less than twenty yards away, with its mate close behind. As it flew past me, it looked at me and cried out to me. An electrifying shock went through me. It was as if God was talking to me through this messenger. I was speechless, excited, and I had no idea what was being said to me. I stood there for some time, dazed and trying to comprehend what I had seen and heard and felt. It all happened so quickly I wasn't prepared. I began to see again the mountains covered with snow and the familiar seagulls. As I stood there, three redhead ducks landed on the river below, and a woodpecker flew to the top of a large dead pine and began tapping away in his own version of the Morse code. I turned and started home filled with a new excitement, a knowledge of God and an appreciation for His world; but what had that call meant?

As Tom puzzled through this experience, the Lord gave me my own puzzle to try to solve. One night deep in the winter I was suddenly awakened with the memory of a startling dream. This dream was not like any other dream I'd ever had. I knew it was not from eating some strange combination for dinner that night. There was a striking reality about this dream.

I dreamed that I was in a long, narrow room with a very low ceiling and a dirt floor. The room was dark, but there was enough light that I could see mammoth spider webs. I could not walk erect because of the low ceiling and the cobwebs. The place smelled musty and moldy and lifeless. I felt contempt. My body was cramped. What a deplorable mess this place was. It gave me the shivers.

Then I heard a voice. It was calling me. "Lois," it said. I had never heard the voice before, and yet it was familiar. I began to make my way through the dark and the cobwebs and over the dirt floor toward that voice. Then I found a doorway that I had not seen before. It was through this doorway that the faint light was coming so that I could see in this dark room. When I got to the doorway, I found there were two steps up from the level of the dirt floor. I stood there hesitating, and I heard the call again, "Lois." I walked up the steps one at a time. I began to stand a little straighter. I saw that I was in a large room with a very high ceiling. The room seemed like a storefront. There were two bay windows for displaying items for sale. There was a door between the windows. The room had a wooden floor and was completely barren except for one shelf on the left wall. It looked wide, almost like a bunk. As I watched, the front door opened, and Jesus came into the room. He slowly walked to the center of the room. There was such a radiance around Him that the whole room filled with light. My heart leaped with joy! Jesus extended His arms toward me. "Lois," He called. It was the voice I had heard! Jesus was calling me! With joy and trembling I started toward Him. With each step the room became brighter, and I felt a strong but gentle warmth pulling me closer. I was nearly ecstatic. But as I was making my way step by step toward Him, I began to feel something around my feet. There were several somethings around my feet. They were alive and furry. They began to jump up on my legs and nip at my feet. My thoughts began to focus on them instead of on Jesus, and yet I did not look away from Him. A great turmoil began to rage in me. If I looked away from Jesus, I knew He would leave. I could not bear to have Him leave. And yet what were these things at my feet? In the corner of my eye I noticed that there was a figure of a person with no face sitting up on the bunk attached to the wall. I realized that whoever it was had sat up as soon as Jesus had come into the room. I began to be afraid of what these things at my feet were. "They must be rats!" I thought. As dirty as that room was where I came from, I was sure there must be all kinds of rats in there. "They've come out here, and they are trying to bite me. I'll probably get rabies and die if they bite me." I began to kick at them, but still I did not look away from Jesus. I could not bear for Him to go away. The "rats" renewed their jumping and nipping, and finally I could not resist it. I looked down. I saw five black, furry kittens clawing at my legs and playing with my toes. I was shocked and yet relieved. I began to realize that the light was becoming less intense in the room, and I looked quickly back to Jesus. He was gone. I ran to where He had been, but He was gone. That's when I woke up.

I lay in the dark night, trembling under the quilts and listening to Tom's steady, quiet breathing. I could make no sense out of my dream, but one thing was sure: I'd heard Christ's voice, and He had been calling me.

21

The third Advent candle was lit, and the third banner was hung. Only one and a half weeks till Christmas. The store presents had arrived by mail on the boat, and I was nearly finished with the gifts I was making. I had knitted sweaters for Tom and Sally and was nearly finished with the one for Amy. I had sewed one outfit apiece for the girls, with fancy handwork on them. I'd even made pajamas. There was only one thing left. We needed a tree. Edith came to our house after work one afternoon, and we all bundled up in boots and warm coats and mittens. We started out across the fields in search of the best tree ever. Tom carried his chain saw, and I lugged along the ax. Sally spied a lovely little tree, so we all waddled through the snow to the tree. It was pretty from the side we had seen, but the other side was flat. So on to the next tree. No that one had a big bare spot. How about that one over by the creek? No it's much too big. Yes and here's a great tree for Charlie Brown. Isn't it pathetic?

At last we found the perfect tree, no flat sides or bare spots and just the right size. Tom cut it down under the excellent advice of the rest of us, and we were soon on our merry way home. The tree was not so heavy as to need five people to carry it, but we all grabbed hold anyway. Tom finally relinquished his end to Edith and was content to carry the saw and ax. Sally and Amy, still wearing her hockey helmet, maneuvered the top end. Over the hill and through the woods we carried our perfect little tree under a sky dark with snow clouds. The air was getting colder by the minute. It would be a good night to be inside trimming a tree by the fireside.

What a joyous night that was! After dinner Tom put the tree in its holder, and we strung it with lights. Then we wound the colorful paper chain that the girls had made. We hung the little wooden ornaments that we had all painted during the evenings since Thanksgiving. We had a few glass ornaments our friend Helen, in Columbus, had given us before she had the stroke. We strung popcorn, in between eating handfuls of it, and wound those chains around our tree. In a great climactic ceremony Tom put the star on top. Our Christmas tree was finished, and nowhere in the world was there a more beautiful one or one decorated with more joy and pride.

We unpacked the crèche and lovingly set it where all could see. Sally had made a precious, tiny crèche, complete with camel and donkey, out of baking soda and salt clay. The shepherds carried staffs that had once been toothpicks, and all the clothing was painted in bright colors. The baby Jesus lay in a tiny yellow manger. We were so pleased with this lovely crèche that it sat in the central place in our household: the middle of the kitchen table.

Amy had cut out yellow construction paper stars, one for each day in Advent. Each evening before she went to bed, we read our Christmas devotions, and she taped another star to the kitchen window. Over and over each day she counted them and then counted the ones left to be hung. How we looked forward to Christmas! And this year there was to be a special treat. Tom's sister and her family were to visit us for a week right after Christmas.

One of my favorite parts of Christmas preparations was hearing Handel's *Messiah*. I longed to hear it this year, as my new relationship with the Lord promised to make this splendid music even more meaningful. But how does one living in the wilderness get to hear Handel's *Messiah*? I could go to Seattle to hear it, but that really was out of the question, even though Tom, knowing how much it would mean to me, had tried to figure some way for me to go. But an exciting thing happened about the time we got the tree up. A notice came in the mail from the mail-order library in Wenatchee saying they had started a cassette tape–lending service. And guess what tape was available? Handel's *Messiah!*

The day it came, I'm afraid I rushed the girls to bed so I could listen without distraction to some of my very favorite music. Tom took his book and cocoa to the bedroom. Handel was not his kind of music. I turned the tape on and cozied down in the leather chair by the crackling fire. Very shortly I was transported from my cabin deep in the wilderness to a magnificent auditorium, hearing a host of beautiful voices singing praises from Scripture to God.

> For unto us a child is born, unto us a son is given: and the government shall be upon his shoulder: and his name shall be called Wonderful, Counsellor, The mighty God, The everlasting Father, The Prince of Peace. (Isa. 9:6)

A surge of great hope ran through me as I heard them proclaim the words in Scripture, "I know that my redeemer liveth" (Job 19:25).

Then the music went on into another part that was unfamiliar to me, and I opened my eyes to look up the verses in my Bible. As I opened the book, a piece of paper fell out. It was the latest letter from my mother. It had not been the usual letter from Mother, and it had news in it that puzzled me. I had needed to think about it, and so I had put it in my Bible. As I picked it up now, I read through it again. It was a beautiful letter of testimony. My mother had been attending a Bible study group for some time and had just recently been there when there had been great discussion on the baptism of the Holy Spirit. She had listened and questioned and then asked to receive the baptism. She described to me what a beautiful experience it had been and how much it had meant in her life already. I was not sure how I felt about that whole experience. I knew my sister had had this experience, but I had discredited it because she had always been inclined to strange things—so I thought. But Mother was not. She was very levelheaded. She was not easily duped into things. I could not discount her experience.

Besides the prompting of this letter, our Bible study sessions kept coming up with questions about the baptism. No one knew any answers. I had read a couple of books about the baptism or infilling of the Spirit, and everyone seemed to agree that it was an experience of freedom and joy and new depth of living in Jesus.

Now I sat up straight. Could it be possible? Could it really be true that there was more to be had in this relationship with Jesus? Yes I was sure that was true. I remembered my dream and the joy I'd felt as I walked toward Him and the emptiness I'd felt when He was gone. But still, maybe this wasn't the way to more fullness in Him. Maybe the way was through more study and prayer. Maybe this experience was really just an emotional work-up or something. To be perfectly honest, I was afraid of it. I was afraid I would fall down on the floor and start talking in a language I didn't know anything about. That would be frightening. And what if I did it sometime in public? That would be embarrassing. I did not want to be a fool. And yet all the while I reasoned, there was a little cry inside of me wanting more of Jesus, wanting to be totally surrendered to Him.

I put the letter down and heard again the music from the tape, which was quoting Revelation 3:20:

> Behold, I stand at the door, and knock: if any man hear my voice, and open the door, I will come in to him, and will sup with him, and he with me.

A longing began to overtake me. To think that I could have a relationship with Jesus like that. He could be so close to me that He would be part of everything I do, even down to eating a meal. To think that I could just sit at the table and talk with Him and share with Him and He with me as the closest possible friend. There's no holding back from a friend like that. There's no room for fear. There is only total acceptance of who He is and what He has to give.

"Behold, I stand at the door, and knock . . . open the door." Those lines rang through my head and heart. Finally I said, "Okay, Lord. I will open the door to You. Come in all the way. I thought I'd done this before when I first accepted You as my Savior, but there seems to be something more, and I want it, even though I am afraid. But I want to open my heart to You anyway."

Nothing happened.

"Behold, I stand at the door, and knock," the people kept on singing. And then I knew I was to go to the front door of our cabin and open it. I nearly laughed.

"Why do I need to do that? It isn't a literal thing. It's symbolic."

"Go to the door and open it so that I may come in." It filled my mind. I even heard a rattling at the door. "It's the wind, I'm sure. It has started to blow a little. Lord, why do I need to go to the door and open it? Haven't I already done it in my heart?"

"Go to the door and open it. It is a physical act that shows your total surrender to Me. Get up and walk across the room and open the door to Me. I am waiting to come fully into your life and give you great joy."

The music went on. The fire danced and crackled as though it wanted to respond. At last I moved my feet from the chair onto the floor. Nothing changed. Then I put the Bible on the side table. Still there was no change, only an urging to go on and the rattling at the door. Slowly I walked across the room and put my hand on the door handle. The rattling stopped. I hesitated.

"Open it. Do not be afraid. I love you. I have only good to give you. Trust Me. Open the door."

Slowly I turned the handle and opened the door. A warm and gentle breeze reached in to me. I stepped out into the December night and was totally enveloped in balmy, sweet breezes that filled me with love. Tears slid down my face as I said in new fullness, "I love You, Father, my Creator. I love You, Jesus, my Redeemer. I love You, Holy Spirit, my Guide and Comforter. I love You, my God. I totally commit myself to You and trust You will give only what is good for me."

I stood in His loving presence for some time, enveloped in His gentle, warm breeze under the cold December stars. There was nothing to be afraid of.

22

Two days after Christmas we were at the landing, waiting for the boat. Janet, Tom's sister, and Richard, her husband, were coming for a week with their two youngest children, Gretchen and Mary. Their two older children, Kathy and Dick, were college age and had other plans for the holidays. They had been with us the previous hunting season, and we'd had a wonderful time. We were sorry they couldn't come with the rest of the family, but we understood.

We had always enjoyed Janet and Richard. Tom had lived with them during part of his college work at Ohio State University. Richard had also been a student at Ohio State, getting his doctorate in nuclear physics. After Richard graduated, they moved to Seattle. We were delighted to be closer to them now. We'd spent Christmas with them the last two years, and they had come to our house in the summers. Richard and the older children had come every hunting season. Now we looked forward to their visit with great joy.

It was a clear winter day as the boat eased into the dock.

"There they are," Sally shouted.

We saw them waving from the upper level. In no time we were hugging and all talking at once. We grabbed their luggage and piled into the old ranch wagon and headed up the valley. They were "ooing" and "ahing" at the sight of the valley in winter. It was beautiful. The snow softened the cragginess of the mountains and smoothed out the rocky shoreline. The blue lake sparkled in the sunlight.

"Gosh that water looks cold," remarked Mary.

"You're right; it is. The lake never freezes because of the depth of it and because we really don't have enough cold weather to freeze more than little places along the edge. But it is still plenty cold."

We turned away from the lake and started up the valley. The road looked much like a bobsled run. It had been cleared enough for one car, and the snow was piled in steep banks along the side.

"What do you do if you meet a car?" Gretchen asked.

"Somebody has to back up," I answered.

"Yeh and Mama doesn't like to either," Sally told on me. "She makes a sad, helpless face if the other person is a man. They usually back up for her. It's a problem if the other driver is a woman."

Everybody laughed.

We passed peaceful little cabins nestled here and there in the snow. Some were empty, with boarded windows. Others had an inviting curl of smoke rising from their chimneys and skis stabbed into the snow by their front doors.

"Look at the deer," Mary shouted, pointing to the edge of a wooded area. "They don't look like they did last summer. Their coats are much heavier, aren't they?"

We were glad to get to our cabin and back up into our slot, the cleared area to park the car near the road. Laps were beginning to get cramped from holding people for five slow miles.

"Oh your house looks so cozy," Janet remarked.

It really did. I was proud of it. It was nestled in the snow beneath the two big trees. A curl of smoke promised it would be warm inside. Our Christmas tree stood at the window, with all our decorations shining. Our Advent banners hung at the top of the other window, giving it a festive look. The side porch was filled with wood that promised warmth in days ahead.

We had a lovely holiday, talking and eating and talking. We read together at night in front of the fire. We went on outings and even rented skis for our guest family from the ski shop at the landing. The kids made snowmen and snowhouses and snow animals and everything else they could think to make out of snow. Everything was a marvelous success except for our one disaster.

One evening, right in the middle of a game being played on the rug in front of the fire, the Christmas tree fell over. There was no warning. It just flopped right over. Richard and Tom picked it up and discovered that one of the legs on the stand had broken. There was no way to make it stand up again. There was nothing to do but take it down. I was so disappointed I cried. It was a somber group that put away the ornaments and carried the tree outside.

Too soon we all piled back into the car to go meet the boat. It had snowed the night before, and what with all the weight in the car, we drug bottom most of the way. The kids in the back seat loved it. Snow kept coming up through the hole in the floor, and they were very willing to redistribute the snow, mostly in each other's faces. We were truly sorry to wave good-bye, but it had been a time to remember.

The next day we decided to go to the dump. We needed to brighten our spirits because we missed our family so much. Besides that we had plenty to go to the dump.

Dump day was always a winter treat. We actually looked forward to it. We burned everything that could be burned at home, and we crushed all the cans and broke the glass containers. When the two garbage cans were filled, we loaded them in the back of the ranch wagon, along with the sled, and headed for the dump.

It was located so that we had to go up a long hill that wound between trees. Of course in the winter there was no way to drive up there. We put one can on the sled and pulled it up. We could have taken both at once, but that would have spoiled the fun. At the top we dumped the stuff into the big hole, and then the fun began. One could pull the sled and can back down the hill, but why not ride down? It was a genuine thrill to race down the hill on the little sled, darting around the trees and often rolling into the snowbank at the bottom. We were sorry we had only two garbage cans to empty.

We took advantage of the slope near the powerhouse, too. It was not really steep, but there was enough incline that we could start there and coast almost all the way home down the seldom-used road.

One of the highlights of winter was the Snow Day held annually at Wendy and Phil's in the old Buckner orchard. On the appointed day cars would line up in every turnaround near the orchard. Then, by ski or snowmobile, we made the trek back into the orchard. It was best not to be the very first because then a ski track had to be made. Of course we didn't want to be too late because parking could be a problem. Packs with games and food bulged on nearly every back. Big pots of stew passed us on the Courtney's snowmobile. By the time we came in sight of the cabin, we were glad to see the fire going, with the promise of warmth and a hot drink.

Snowmobiles were parked in front, and many pairs of skis stood upright in the snow by the front door.

We laughed and talked and played games and ate. We sang and knitted and rocked the little ones to sleep. There was always a middle-of-the-afternoon ski trek through the orchard and meadow areas, ending at the short but steep hill that turned cross-country skis into downhill skis.

One year the men dug horseshoe pits out of the snow. It was hilarious to see the men step down into the pits and sling the horseshoes over the snow to a destination they had to have difficulty seeing. Even when it began to snow, they continued until they had a champion.

There was more food and hot drinks, and just before dark we waved a fond farewell and started back to our cars and home.

For all its inconvenience the winter was really a joyful time.

23

To write, or not to write. That was my question.

Since I was in high school, I had been interested in writing. I'd gotten good grades on compositions, and they were usually read to the class as good examples of something or other. But when I went to college, it was a different story. In freshman English my first composition was read to the class—but as an example of how not to write.

I had written a story about Tom's and my first swimming date. He and his family lived on a lake, and shortly after I met him, he asked me to come to a swimming party there. I loved to swim, but a person has to wear a bathing suit at a swimming party. If I wore a bathing suit, Tom would very clearly see my scoliosis and my atrophied leg. I really liked Tom. He was fun to be with, nice to me, and so handsome. It was a difficult decision to make. If I said no, he might ask another girl. That scared me. But if I said yes, he would see my body for what it was. What if that made him change his mind about me before he ever really got to know me? As the freshman theme told, I decided to go. Tom did see my limitations: the scoliosis, the shriveled leg, and the scars both physical and emotional. There was nothing he could do about the physical scars, but his warm smile and quick hug did wonders for my emotional scars. Before we left the party, he asked if he could pick me up at school the next day. Then I knew he really didn't mind me not looking like a beauty queen.

I displayed all my fears in that freshman theme and Tom's (now my fiancé) loving response, and the theme was read as an example of sickening-sweet, confessional-type writing, which was obviously detested by the instructor. Her reactions and attitude put my desire to write back down in the cellar. It was not only the writing; it was the emotion that she had rejected. How could I write without expressing my feelings? I couldn't, so I guessed I couldn't write.

Several years later in Stehekin I found the courage to enroll in a short story course. It was by correspondence from the University of Washington in Seattle. That was a pretty safe distance. There would be no class to hear my stories either. Although the professor provoked much thought in me, I never felt attacked. And I did learn a great deal. The mail-order library was very obliging and sent me book after book on how to write. I devoured them all. But the greatest thing was when I got a story back and the professor had written on it, "Before you send this out, I suggest you might want to change. . . ." I never saw what he thought I should change. My eyes and hopes stuck on that first "Before you send this out." He seemed to expect that I would send it to a publisher, which meant that he seemed to think my writing was worthwhile. He thought it was okay for me to express feelings, although I was very careful that my feelings were masked as the feelings of the people in my stories. I never sent the story out, but I basked in his apparent confidence in my writing. My A in the course confirmed his opinion.

Maybe I really could be a writer. All the books had said that to be a writer, a person had to write—lots and often. There was little opportunity for me to write in the summer months because of camp and other guests, so I decided that winter would be my writing time. I began to work at it. One major thing resulted. I became a perfectly horrible grouch. If anyone interrupted me, I bit their head off. The housework often did not get done as it should have because I would run to my desk by the window looking into the woods and scribble about someone's dramatic encounter with life.

Finally I began to hear the Holy Spirit convicting me. One night in February, after everyone else was asleep, I cried to my Lord.

"Lord, I thought you had given me a talent for writing. I know you expect us to use the talents you give us, and I do want to use it. But, Lord, it just isn't working. I'm so ugly to the girls when they interrupt me. O Lord, I love them so much. Why do I run them away from me? They're only children, and they have needs to be met. And, Lord, look at this house. I don't even seem to attempt to keep it straight. Lord, I guess I'll just have to give up writing." A pain went through me. "Maybe this writing thing is really Satan's way of disrupting our home. Maybe I just shouldn't do it now. I need Your guidance, Lord. If You want me to write, have someone ask me to write something specifically, and have them tell me where to send it. Then I'll know You want me to write it." That seemed like a good check, but how long might I have to wait for directions? Quickly I added to my proposal, "And Lord, make it come within the next two weeks."

I put the writing material away but within easy reach, just in case I'd need them quickly, and I waited. The first week passed, and the mail carried no requests for my talents. I worried through the second week. My family seemed relieved at my new attitude, and they definitely liked the more orderly household. I had shared with Tom what my "fleece" was with the Lord. He anxiously watched the mail, too. At the end of two weeks nothing had come. There was not even anything I could misconstrue into a directive. Once more I talked with my Lord.

"Well, Lord, I guess I was wrong. I'm taking this two weeks' silence as direction that You don't want me to write. Gosh, Lord, I really do want to do it. Just think how I could write stories about You. I could tell people about You, and they would come to You and let You save them. Wouldn't that be wonderful, Lord?"

There was nothing but silence.

I was more than a little deflated; I was flat. But I had a clear direction. I'd asked for it, and I got it. In tears I relinquished all my hopes of being a writer.

"Okay, Lord. I love You more than I love writing. I'll do what You say. Take it, Lord. Take my writing. You keep it for me. I don't want it till You want me to have it. And if that's never, well, okay."

My heart was breaking as I gave it all up. Or almost all of it.

"Lord, if you ever want me to write anything, just ask me. Tell me exactly what to write and where to send it."

Life went back to normal—whatever that is—at our house. I put all the writing materials in a place that was very difficult to reach. I was through with it unless I got specific instructions from the Lord.

Six weeks later we got a letter from our former pastor in Ohio, Dr. William E. Smith. Last October I had written to him in some detail about Amy's ordeal. We had received several letters from him in the meantime, and he never had mentioned my writing talents. But this letter was very clear. He said, "I've been meaning to tell you, Lois, that I think you should write up the story of Amy's ordeal and your faith through it and send the story to *Guideposts* magazine." He went on to give his reasons, but I didn't really notice. There was a specific request for a specific story and directions on where to send it.

I had thought that if a directive ever came to write, I would jump and holler and tear off to the typewriter. Instead I was filled with a calm. I smiled and put the letter back in the envelope and went about my household chores. When Tom came home from school, he read it.

"Well, Sweetie Pie, there it is. That's pretty specific. Want me to get your writing things out?"

"Sure, but there's no hurry. Let's have dinner first."

He was astounded at my nonchalance.

For the next three days, whenever a minute arose that I was not needed, I sat down at the desk and wrote. The house was in perfect order. If one of the children or Tom needed anything, I eagerly helped them. There was no pressure or urgency about the writing. The thing that really amazed me was that whenever I was interrupted and then returned to the writing, I was able to start right where I had left off. I instantly remembered what I had planned to say. It was a beautiful experience, an extreme opposite to my previous writing attempts. I couldn't help laughing with the Lord.

"I see now, Lord. When it is for You, You make it happen, and without problems for other people. I'll remember that, Lord. I'll only write under Your specific directions." I smiled broadly. "Anyway that's the only way I can write. I gave my talent to You, so I can't use it if You don't give it back to me. I guess You won't give it to me without telling me how to use it."

With great peace and quiet excitement I mailed the story to *Guideposts*. It came back within a week: wrong address. I had used an old magazine to get the address. I found the new address and sent it off the second time.

During the next month I seldom thought of it. It was the Lord's, and He would take care of it. When the letter of acceptance came from the publisher, I was not really surprised. I was very excited but not really surprised.

"We did it, didn't we, Lord? We're a terrific pair, You and I. This is fun to work with You. You're a fantastic boss. Holler when You want to do it again. It's strictly up to You."

I would learn again that the writing truly is up to Him.

24

"Hey! Anybody home?"

"Sure is. I'm here," I called as I pulled the needle through the quilt and pushed my chair back from the quilt frame. "I'm coming."

I went to the side door and found Wally, a longtime resident of the valley. He stood at the door, looking down at something in his cupped hand.

"What do you have, Wally?" I asked, going out onto the porch.

"Found this hummingbird laying on the shop floor. Must have been in there all night. I don't think it's dead, but I ain't got time to mess with it. You want it?"

"Well, sure. But what should I do with it?" I looked at the tiny bird Wally gently placed in my hand. It looked pretty pathetic. Its eyes were closed, and its claws were drawn up against its light belly. Its rufous-colored head flopped backward, and the only sign of life was the faint movement of the flaming red throat and chest.

"See if you can get it to eat. Take your feeder there"—he pointed at the hummingbird feeder attached to the house—"and poke his beak into the tube. Maybe a little bit will trickle into his beak. That's 'bout all you can do."

As Wally walked back to the woodshop, I took the bird in one hand and the feeder in the other and sat in the shade under a maple tree. It was May, and the days were getting warmer. The snow was gone, and spring was busy awakening all the winter sleepers. It was very pleasant under the tree, and I sat there for some time, talking quietly to the bird and sticking the tube of the feeder over his beak. Amy woke from her nap and came out to join us. "Look, Mommy! He's sticking his tongue out!" she shouted after a while. Sure enough, we could see the tiny, tubelike tongue darting into the sugar-and-water solution.

"It looks like a straw, Mommy," Amy observed.

"You're right. And he uses it like a straw. He sucks the sugar water with his tongue."

By the time Sally and Tom came home from school, our "baby" was standing up in my hand and looking around. He still wanted frequent sips from the feeder. The four of us were gathered round, staring at him and remarking about what beautiful creatures God had made, when the bird suddenly flapped his wings at us as if he was waving. Then, with a humming sound, he rose straight up like a helicopter and sat on the limb of the tree. Tom hung the feeder back on the house, and we watched as the bird made several trips to the feeder and returned to the tree branch. Finally he whizzed off around the side of the house and was gone.

Soon it was June again. As I crawled along the ground, I felt the warm sun on my back and the moist, cool earth under my legs. I was setting out the small plants we had started weeks before in the cabin. I stopped for a moment, and settling back on my heels, I surveyed our garden. We had expanded it this spring. This back garden ran from the very edge of the woods and was about twenty-five by forty-five feet. In it we planned to have cabbage, broccoli, beets, cauliflower, carrots, potatoes, bush beans, lettuce, tomatoes, and a few rows of corn. We were planting onions, garlic, marigolds, and nasturtiums around the edges to discourage the little creatures of the woods from getting too interested in the garden. Here and there I planted some daisy seeds just because I like daisies. At the side of the house we had a strawberry patch and a pea patch, with carrots in between the rows of peas. In front of the cabin, where most homeowners have shrubs, we planted a row of bush beans, then a row of broccoli, then a row of beets, and finally a row of marigolds with onions interspersed. It was really quite lovely, as well as practical.

We all four prepared the garden areas, planted the seeds, kept the weeds out, watered regularly. Sally and Amy also had their own garden areas, where they planted whatever and however they chose. It was a source of enjoyment and accomplishment, as well as a source of food for now and for the winter. There was only one problem: animals.

How does one living and gardening in the wilderness keep wild animals out of the garden? A fence, right? We all four went into the woods and cut small dead trees and cut them in six-foot lengths. By burying them a foot, we would still have a five-foot fence. We dug holes at the proper distances and sunk the poles. We had written downlake for fencing to be sent to stretch between the posts. But no fencing came. Finally we had Ernie, the pilot, call the store for us. They were very sorry, but they had no fencing, and they didn't think they would be getting any. Ernie graciously called other stores, but the information was always the same: No fencing was available. We were devastated. How could we possibly protect this garden without a fence? Some of the other people in the valley had fencing from previous years. Others were building tall picket fences. Tom was not interested in doing that because the property was not his and there was always the possibility that we would be leaving the valley someday.

One evening during our fencing crisis, Tom and I were working in the big garden, and the girls were busy in theirs. A lovely family had moved in nearby for the season, and they had a dog. The dog was very friendly and very large. As soon as she saw us, she came tearing over to the children.

"Get away," they screeched. "You're stepping on the plants. Daddy! Mommy!" they wailed.

We raced to their rescue only to have the dog tear through our garden, breaking off one tiny plant after another. I must admit my attitude and even my shouts were not of a saintly kind. We had to find fencing to save the garden from the dog, if not from the "wild" animals.

I felt very silly wrapping string around those fine wooden fence posts. String wouldn't keep a chipmunk out. But I was determined to put something up, and string was all we had.

That evening I had time to think and pray about the problem. I was rereading and working on the materials Tom had gotten at the Basic Youth Conflicts Seminar. It just happened that I had come to the section that discussed the relinquishment of our things to God. These things really did not belong to us. They actually were God's. I began to understand that I needed to apply this to the gardens.

"Tom," I said, "those gardens are not ours."

"What do you mean?" he asked.

"Well, we dug them and took all the grass and stuff out. We hoed the ground until it was fine. Then we planted seeds or small plants. But it's not our garden."

"I see what you mean," he said. "We may have done all that work, but there's nothing we can do to make the seed grow. Only God can do that. So it's His garden, right?"

"Exactly. There's no way we can make it grow, and there's no way we can protect it. We've tried every way we can short of splitting slats."

Tom got up, took my hand, and led me outside. We stood by the back garden.

"Lord," Tom said, "this is Your garden. You made the soil. We've just worked it a little. You made the seeds. We just put them in the ground. You have total control over whether or not they grow. You also have complete control over whether or not they reach maturity. We think we need this food, Lord, but You know whether or not we do. Lord, we can't protect this garden from anything—bugs, rabbits, dogs, deer, or bears. But You can if You choose to. It's up to You, Lord. It's Yours. Do what You want with it."

From that day on it was an adventure to see what would happen to the wilderness garden protected by only a string fence.

We were busy seeing new beginnings in other areas of our valley life. The many hours of work that Bruce Groseclose had put in over the fall and winter had paid off. The first Sunday of June we were going to have a minister conduct a real worship service for us! There had been several meetings in the valley to provide our input, and Bruce had kept us posted on how things were going at the other end of the lake. With Bruce's help we organized the Stehekin Community Church. Darrell Wilsey was elected the president of the group, and Tom was the secretary-treasurer. Bruce arranged for ministers of several denominations to come to Stehekin for a weekend and hold services. Our group agreed to pay the transportation uplake and to provide housing and meals. We would be meeting in the Wilsey's living room because it seemed to be large enough and was located closest to the landing. It was a very excited little group of Christians that met the boat bringing their first weekend pastor. We took turns having the pastors stay in our homes. It was exciting to have them in our house, yet it was a little scary, too. We hadn't even talked with a pastor for years, and here one was staying with us. I was a bit self-conscious about my behavior and the children's, and about my housekeeping and cooking. But the guests were always more than gracious and seemed to enjoy their visits. We had many very interesting discussions in the evening and really learned more around the dinner table or over coffee after the girls were in bed than we learned in the services.

In July we moved the services into the old Golden West Lodge. We were having about thirty people at the services because tourists were also attending. A piano was found and moved to the old lodge; a table with a beautiful tablecloth served as the communion table. Someone made a lovely wooden cross; candles appeared; an open Bible and flowers from someone's garden or wild flowers completed the worship center. A huge stone fireplace provided the backdrop many mornings, as a fire was often needed to warm the large old lobby. But we were very pleased. Our "church" was simple and rustic as were our lives, and yet it was beautiful.

The services were uncomplicated, too. One of our men led the singing, and his wife played the piano, often with one or two of their four pre-school children on the bench beside her. We prayed and shared God's blessings in our lives, and we listened as the one He sent to us for that week gave us a message or lesson.

I will never forget the day a visitor stood up and said, "May I sing for you and the Lord?" We assured him that we'd love it and that no doubt the Lord would, too. He put his guitar strap over his shoulder and stood in front of us but turned a little so that he could look out the windows and across the lake at the mountains and trees.

There was a hush over the old lobby as he began to strum his guitar. As he started to sing, goose bumps popped up on my skin. What a beautiful voice he had, yes. But to hear what he was singing!

> *Oh Lord my God! When I in awesome wonder*
> *Consider all the worlds* Thy hands have made,*
> *I see the stars, I hear the rolling* thunder,*
> *Thy power throughout the universe displayed,*
> *Then sings my soul, my Savior God to Thee:*
> *How great Thou art, how great Thou art!*
> *Then sings my soul, my Savior God to Thee:*
> *How great Thou art, how great Thou art!*

Every eye looked out the windows, and every heart was warmly moved as he sang the second verse.

> *When through the woods and forest glades I wander*
> *And hear the birds sing sweetly in the trees,*
> *When I look down from lofty mountain grandeur*
> *And hear the brooks and feel the gentle breeze,*
> *Then sings my soul, my Savior God to Thee:*
> *How great Thou art, how great Thou art!*
> *Then sings my soul, my Savior God to Thee:*
> *How great Thou art, how great Thou art!*

Tom and I clutched each other's hand tightly as we joined the group in singing the rest of the hymn.

By July we realized we needed to make other housing arrangements for the ministers because they wanted to bring their families with them and make a short vacation out of the trip. Once more Bruce came to the rescue. He found a group willing to buy a camping trailer for the church to use for the visiting ministers and their families. He even found an individual who sent a car up on the barge for the ministers to use.

Before the trailer arrived, there was much discussion about where it could be parked and have the necessary hookups. There turned out to be only one acceptable place: a lot about one hundred yards from our house. In times past a trailer had been parked there, and the hookups could very easily be put in usable repair. I must admit my first thoughts were not very gracious. I resented sharing my territory with another "house." But there was no other workable alternative. So the trailer came to be next door to us, and with it came a very clear benefit for us that the Lord, in His wisdom, had designed.

Nearly all the ministers who came had never been in Stehekin. Many had never been in any place like it and were not exactly comfortable with the idea of roaming around the area by themselves. They were more than willing to explore if they had a guide. Sally became a first-class preacher's guide. She took them on rigorous walks, showing them where they could fish or find berries or see whatever they asked to see.

The evenings found the minister and his wife comfortably settled in our living room with tall glasses of "sun tea" (a delicious, slowly brewed tea made by teabags and water sitting in the sun all day). We shared far into the night about their experiences in seminary and in the work of pastoring. We were given a view of the ministry that we had never realized before. It seemed, that summer and the next, that there was a constant procession of ministers filing through our house and our lives. It had exciting consequences for our lives, although at the time we were not aware of God's plan behind it all.

The weekly Bible study continued that summer, and invariably the subject of the Holy Spirit came up. No matter what we started out discussing, we ended up on that subject. One stormy evening the group pulled up in front of our cabin, and Maria Byrd ran ahead to us.

"I brought two guests tonight," she said. "They are staying at the lodge for a few days, and we've had many interesting conversations. I think they were sent here by the Lord."

We were introduced to Alan and Kathy and were just beginning our session when it began to pour rain. I remembered I had laundry on the line, so I raced out back. Maria and Sally came with me. I was intent on getting the nearly dry clothes down when Maria shouted, "Look, Lois and Sally. Look at the mountains over there."

We looked up into the falling rain and saw a breathtaking sight. Silhouetted against the dark rain clouds and across the mountains was a double rainbow. We stood in silent awe, the clothes hanging limply in our hands and the summer rain splashing in our faces.

I heard Maria whispering and saw that she was praying. I could not understand her words, but the joy in her face expressed her feelings.

I began to feel wet, so I grabbed the rest of the clothes and ran toward the house. Sally and Maria came after me, shouting to the others to come out and look. It was not nearly as bright when they saw it, but somehow it seemed to us to be a glorious sign from God that this night would be a night we would not forget.

Edith helped me spread the damp clothes on the bed, and then we all settled down again to our Bible study. Without any of our designing the discussion once again turned to the Holy Spirit. There were nine of us present that night, four of whom had knowledge and experience with the baptism of the Holy Spirit. Before the evening was over, we all had knowledge, and some of us had the experience. Alan quietly and with confidence answered all our questions, both from his experience and from the Scriptures. At last he said, "Do any of you wish to receive the baptism of the Spirit?"

"I do," I responded quietly. I was no longer afraid since my experience last winter. As a matter of fact I suspected I'd already received this infilling. But just in case I hadn't, I wanted to make sure.

Tom and another man also responded. Alan spoke with joy, assuring us of the good gifts that God was going to give us. Maria began to pray inaudibly, as did Kathy and Grandma Byrd. Alan put his hands on my shoulders and asked me if I had accepted

Jesus as my Savior. I answered, "Yes." He asked me if I wanted to receive the fullness of the Spirit that Jesus had promised to give us. I said, "Yes." Then Alan prayed very simply that Jesus would send His Spirit on me and fill me with it. I waited with expectation. The room was quiet except for the snap of the low-burning fire and the whispered prayers of the other people.

Slowly a calmness began to sweep through me, a warmth, a freshness, a confidence, an overwhelming love, a promise kept, a joy, a radiance, a peace. I wanted to laugh and to cry. I wanted to sit very still and feel every feeling, and yet I wanted to dance for joy. I wanted to listen intently, for I could almost hear God's presence, and yet I wanted to sing great psalms of praise.

"Abba, Abba," I whispered with joy. "Abba, Abba." And then I realized I was calling the Father by the name Jesus had called Him. I was calling Him "Daddy!"

Tom also experienced a new level of commitment and joy that was manifested daily in new attitudes and actions. The other man seemed to have a new experience with the Lord also.

After everyone had gone home, I stood in the wet grass outside, watching the clouds race past the moon. I didn't want the night to end. I wanted this joy to go on forever.

"Is this feeling like it is in heaven?" I asked my Lord.

I felt Him smile. "Yes, only more so."

More? How could it be? I would surely burst if one more drop of joy fell on me.

25

"You know what?" Tom spoke quietly.

It was shortly before our Stehekin Summer session was to begin. It was evening, and Tom was sitting at the kitchen table, looking out the window at the twilight. I thought he was watching the deer at the salt lick. I was busy at the sink, washing the first vegetables from the garden.

"What?" I answered going right ahead with the vegetables.

He continued looking out the window and said quietly, "I think I might like to be a—" He paused as though he wasn't sure he could even say it. Then he continued barely above a whisper, "—a youth minister."

I wasn't sure I'd heard him. I put down the knife and turned off the water. "A what?" I asked.

He turned around in the chair and faced me. "A youth minister. A minister of youth."

I was shocked. I simply could not comprehend what he had said.

"A what?" I asked again.

Tom smiled. Then he chuckled. "Sounds crazy, doesn't it? Me, a minister." Then the chuckle wasn't enough. He laughed right out loud. And for some strange reason I thought I heard God laughing, too. But He wasn't laughing the way Tom was. There was no tone of incredibility in God's laugh. He was laughing for joy. He was laughing out of sheer happiness and delight.

Still I was speechless. I just stood there, holding a radish. Tom got up and put his arm around me.

"Oh, don't mind me. You know I've always got some kind of a crazy idea. Guess I've been listening to those preachers too much. Just forget I said anything. Okay?" He started toward the door. "Think I'll go take a walk. Bye."

I stood looking at the empty doorway, and then I turned back to my vegetables. I was washing some soil off a radish when I suddenly remembered something that had happened years ago. I had not thought of it since.

We were living in Columbus, Ohio. Sally was about eighteen months old, and we had just moved into our first unrented home. We had occasionally attended a church nearby. This particular Sunday Sally was sick. Tom gladly offered to stay home with her if I wanted to go to church by myself. I was not that faithful, but for some reason I decided to go. When I got there, I had to sit in the balcony because all the seats on the main floor were taken. When I opened the bulletin and saw that it was Confirmation Sunday, I was sorry I had made the effort to come. I really wasn't very interested in seeing all these kids become members of the church. Besides that would mean the sermon would be for them, and so it really wouldn't mean much to me. But I was stuck. I couldn't very well get up and walk out; besides the processional had started. I stood and sang the hymn and resigned myself to a not too interesting hour. Soon the youth minister, Louis Buckalew, stepped up to the pulpit and began talking about the confirmands and the program they had gone through to prepare for today. I knew the youth minister fairly well because he was also the pastor who was involved with the young married couples' group. Tom and I occasionally attended their socials. As I watched and listened, an amazing thing happened. Right before my eyes Lou changed into Tom. It was no longer Lou in the pulpit, recommending these young people for church membership. It was my husband, Tom. It was incredible. I looked around to see if anyone else was shocked. Nobody seemed to notice the difference. I shook my head and blinked my eyes a few times and looked back at the pulpit. There stood Tom. Wow! I was sure I was losing my mind! It was just plain creepy. Well no one else seemed to notice, so I pretended that I didn't either. Then I heard a voice inside say, "This is where your husband belongs." Once more I rolled my eyes around to see if anyone else had heard this ridiculous statement. Tom wasn't even a Christian really. Oh he went to church sometimes, but he really couldn't be called a Christian. If he saw Jesus on the street, he would have tipped his hat to Him, but that's about as much of a relationship as they had. I had a bit of a problem settling back into the service. It had been quite a shocking experience, one that I had never told anyone. Maybe I was going crazy. I sure didn't want anyone to know it. At least not yet. So I forgot about it myself. Not until that evening in Stehekin did I remember it.

I went to the door. I could see Tom walking across the meadow. I remembered that winter night when he was on his way to the Bible study. "Lord, what are You telling me? Do You really want Tom to be a minister?"

26

"Who cares what the Bible says? Why does God always have to have His way?" The teenage girl shouted her questions at me. She was one of our campers, and we were walking along the river in the summer twilight. We had, minutes before, had a Bible study and discussion at the cabin as part of their Christian camping experience. This girl had become very agitated, and so we had decided to take a walk after the discussion had concluded. Another girl had decided to come with us, and the third camper had remained at the cabin, sitting under a tree and talking with Tom. Our camp was very small this year, but we were not disturbed. We had asked the Lord to send the young people He wanted to come. These three came, and we grew to love them dearly.

"God *doesn't* always have to get His way. We can choose not to do things the way He wants. We are not little robots whirling and turning at His every whim. We are made in His image, which means in part that we have unlimited creative potential. When we accept reconciliation with God, through Jesus, our capacities are multiplied a millionfold because we begin to grow into the persons God created us to be. Besides God is not some giant celestial party pooper. He just has a bigger view of things than we do. He knows the long-range effects of our thoughts and actions. He can see around the curves in the road. He even knows where the road ends. And you know that God *is* love. He doesn't just love; He is love. He has a great storehouse of good gifts to give us. In the Book of Malachi it says that God wants to open for us the windows of heaven and pour out for us blessings so abundant that there won't even be enough room to hold them. But we can't receive all those blessings if we don't give ourselves to Him and align ourselves with His channel."

We had stopped walking, and the girls were looking out across the river. They were quiet, each deep in her own thoughts.

One girl, Isa, turned to me and said barely above a whisper, "What if you don't like what He gives you?"

I looked out across the river for a while. Finally I said, "There is that possibility. I guess I'll just have to trust Him to give me what's best for me. I guess I have to be willing to take the best instead of the 'goodest,' if you know what I mean. When I was a kid, I always wanted lollipops because they tasted good, much better than the green vegetables and other foods I was given to eat. But, you see, a steady diet of only what tasted good to my childish opinion was not what would make me grow into wholeness and healthy maturity. A continued diet of sweetness wasn't what was best for me."

A cool breeze was blowing off the river, and I began to get very chilly.

"I think I'll go back now. I'm getting cold. You come when you're ready."

As I retraced my steps homeward, I rejoiced with the Lord.

"Thank You, Lord, for these girls. I see why You chose them to be here. Remember, Lord, the night before they came, I got so scared? I was afraid that I wouldn't be able to lead the studies right. I was afraid I wouldn't be able to answer their questions. Remember how I sat outside that night in my nightgown, pouring out my fears to You? I was there a long time, and You didn't answer me. I went back to bed, and as soon as I lay down, my mind was filled with this statement, 'All you need to do is make the Scriptures available to them. I will do the rest.' What a great God You are! And how You have kept Your word. Once more, Lord, I put these beautiful girls in Your hands. Draw them to You, Lord, in the way and time that is best for them."

The next day we were all up early, making the final preparations for their five-day backpacking trip into the mountains. Amid great excitement and laughter Sally and Amy and I drove them to the trail head and waved them off. Tom was in the lead, and Edith was the rear guard. Sally often went on the trips with them. She was a strong hiker and had carried her own pack since she was six years old. Tom had taken her on their first trip together then, and they had gone about five miles up the Lake Shore Trail. Amy was a good hiker, too. She carried a little soft pack with pajamas, socks, and M&M's candies—all the necessities as far as she was concerned. I usually went along on the first trip, which was always a short, easy one for my sake, in order to help the campers learn their camping and cooking skills. But this trip was to be too long and strenuous for the three of us.

Three days later Sally was spending the day with a friend, and Amy was outside playing in the playhouse in the maple tree. I was sewing a blouse for Sally and irrigating the garden. We had dug small trenches between the rows of vegetables, and we watered the garden by filling those trenches. It took exactly ten minutes to fill one trench, so I would move the hose to a new trench, go into the house, set the timer for ten minutes, and sew until the timer rang for me to change the hose again. Shortly after I had started the water into the fourth trench, there was a knock on the door. I looked up to see a summer park ranger at the door.

"Hello," I called. "Come on in."

He stepped cautiously inside. "Mrs. Olson, ah—" He hesitated, looking down at his shoes.

I waited.

"Mrs. Olson," he said quickly, "there's an emergency message for you at the landing."

"Emergency?" I was alarmed. "Is it from Tom? Has something happened on their trip?"

"No. It isn't from your husband. It's from your brother."

"From Joe?"

"Yes. You are to call him right away."

"Okay. Ah—I'll go right now."

"Would you like me to drive you down?" he asked.

"No thank you. I'll need to take my car in order to get back home."

He left, and I called to Amy. "Amy, come quick. Hurry. We need to go right now."

Amy raised the low-hanging branch of the tree and peeked from under it. "Where, Mommy?"

"To the landing. Come, quick," I called as I headed toward the car.

Amy ran behind me. I was in the car, starting it, by the time she got in. "Why, Mommy? What's wrong?"

Before I could answer, she began to scream. She had closed the door on her leg. I turned off the motor and went around to her side of the car to tend the hurt leg. Finally we were on our way toward the landing.

As I drove along the winding road, I kept thinking, "Wonder what it is? Maybe something's happened to Mother. She's been pretty sick lately with her gallbladder. Maybe Joe just wants to tell me she's in the hospital. Maybe the doctor has decided to operate."

I drove a little farther. "Maybe it isn't anything like that. Maybe it's just my crazy brother. Maybe he wants to come see us and wants to know how to get here. He called me plenty of times back in Ohio in the middle of the night just to talk." I tried to convince myself that there was no reason to worry.

The road came out of the woods and wound along the side of the lake. Amy was on her knees, watching for the baby mallard ducks that lived along here. "Slow down, Mommy. I can't see the ducks."

As I slowed down, I felt the car fill with a calmness. I knew it was the Lord. In my mind I heard Him say, "This is part of life. Don't worry. I am with you."

For the remaining distance to the landing I felt assured but very puzzled. "This is part of life. What does that mean?"

When we got to the landing, Amy saw the Wilseys' daughter, who was Amy's age. They ran off together up the hill toward Debbie's house. I went into the coffee shop. Randi was behind the counter. I knew her well. She and many of the summer employees of the lodge came to the Bible studies and to the church services.

"What can I do you for?" she asked, smiling.

"I understand there is an emergency message for me."

"Oh! Well it would be upstairs in the office. I think Mr. Byrd is up there. He'll help you."

I went back outside, around to the back of the building and up the stairs to the office from which Bob and Hilda Byrd and their family managed the lodge area. Both Bob and Maria, his daughter, were there.

"Hello, Lois," Bob said quietly, betraying his concern. "Here, sit down." He pushed a chair toward me. "I'll make the call now. I've turned the radio's speaker on so that you can hear both sides of the conversation."

It took a while to get the call through. This new radiotelephone was quite a deal. It was a radio at our end, but it hooked into the regular telephone system in Wenatchee. Bob was able to talk with people all over the world. There were only two problems. Because we were speaking through a radio, we could not talk and listen at the same time. We had to click on and off. This was in the days before the CB radios were the in thing, and few people understood the need for us to click on and off. The other problem was that because it was a radio, anyone on this frequency could hear everything that was said. It was a long way from a private line.

Finally the call got through, but the line was busy. We waited several minutes and tried again. This time my sister-in-law answered. My brother had married her after I left Florida, so I had never met her and didn't really know her. When she realized who was calling—it took her a minute to understand because Bob was doing the talking for me since I was not a radio operator—she hesitated a minute and finally said, "I think you'd better call back when Joe is here. He'll be back in half an hour. He's over at your uncle's now."

So I waited. I walked around the landing, thinking, wondering, and praying. At last I was sitting by the speaker again, and Joe's voice was coming out of it.

"Can't I talk to her myself?"

Bob patiently explained again what the setup was. He assured Joe that I was next to the speaker and could hear everything he said.

"Well, okay, but I sure wish I could talk to her directly." He hesitated. Maybe he was hoping things would change. Finally I heard him take a deep breath. "Lois." His voice was quivering. "Lois, can you hear me?"

"Yes she can hear you very well," Bob assured him. "Go ahead."

It was quiet except for Joe's breathing. "Lois." The agony in his voice broke my heart. I looked at Maria, and she took my hand. Finally he said it. "Daddy died last night." His voice broke into sobs. I sat stone-still. "Daddy's dead, Lois. He's dead."

How I longed to take Joe in my arms and comfort him. But how could I comfort a voice coming out of a box?

I looked at Bob. "Tell him—tell him—tell him I love him, would you please?"

"Joe," Bob said, "Lois says—she says she loves you."

The sobbing quieted down. "I love her, too," he was able to say.

"Ask him what happened to Daddy, would you please?"

Then began a strange conversation, with one end of it being relayed. We found out that Mother had had a very bad gall-bladder attack. Daddy was out of town on a job, so a neighbor had taken Mother to the hospital. A call was made to him, and he came right away. He was with her that evening and said that he would return the next morning. He did not return. By early afternoon, Florida time, he had not come, so Mother had made some calls. Yes the car was there in the driveway. No, no one had seen Daddy that day. Yes they would get the manager of the mobile home park to go in the house and see if he was all right. They found him dead on the bed. A heart attack.

"How's Mother?" I asked through Bob.

"I don't know. I haven't seen her yet. I'm about ready to drive to Orlando now to see her. [Joe lived in Tampa.] The neighbor just called me to tell me about an hour ago. Maybe Mother doesn't even know yet. I called for you right away. Sara [our sister] doesn't know yet. She's not at home. Nobody answers the phone. Lois"—his voice began to quiver again—"will you come, Lois? We need you here."

"She says she'll try," Bob relayed. "She says it may take a while because Tom is off in the mountains on a trip. But she'll come as soon as she can. She'll let you know what arrangements she can make. And, Joe, she says she loves you very much."

My first tears came when I heard him say back, "I know. I love her, too—and so did Daddy."

Thank God for Bob. How would I have managed without him? He began to think for me. He made no decisions, but he did the thinking and offered me the alternatives. The first thing we needed to do was to tell Tom. Ernie's plane was at the dock, and Jim, who was helping Ernie with all the extra summer flights, was in the coffee shop. With someone to drop a message to Tom, Jim could fly up to where I knew Tom and the campers were. Maria went to get Jim while Bob handed me a paper to write out the message to Tom.

What should I say? How does one write a note saying her father is dead? How can I tell Tom when I can't be there to comfort him? Thank You, God, that Edith is with him. She will help him. I need to tell him that I'm all right. He will be worried about me. How can I say all this? At last I began to write.

> Dearest Tom,
>
> Joe called to tell us that Daddy died last night. A heart attack. Mother is in the hospital with a gallbladder attack. Can you come out tomorrow?
> "In everything give thanks, for this is the will of God in Christ Jesus."
>
> I love you—Lois 3:30 P.M.

Bob was making copies on his small copy machine when Darrell appeared at the door. His face was full of compassion.

"I'm sorry, Lois," was all he said, but that was more than adequate.

I nodded and looked down at my hands. I couldn't look at his eyes anymore. Mine were beginning to be blurry.

Three copies of my letter to Tom were made, and each one was put into a special holder with a long, bright yellow cloth tail attached to it. The holder was weighted so that it would drop to the ground when it was thrown from the plane. The yellow tail would help the people on the ground see it.

I sat on the steps while I waited for Jim and Darrell to return with the news that Tom had gotten the message. Hilda, Bob's wife, brought me a large glass of iced tea. She sat with me for a while. When she had to leave to go back to her work in the restaurant, Randi came out. We didn't talk, but I knew that I was surrounded by caring people. It was enough.

Danny, Darrell's seventh-grader son, came and spoke quietly, "Is there anything I can do for you, Mrs. Olson?" I was very touched by his offer.

Time passed slowly. The afternoon was quiet. Few people were out and moving around in the July heat. I watched a big black carpenter ant crawl up and down the steps several times. I listened to the waves of the lake lapping rhythmically at the dock and dishes clattering in the restaurant kitchen. Perspiration trickled down my chest. I didn't see Amy. Darrell must have asked Betty, his wife, to keep Amy for a while.

At last I heard the drone of the plane. It landed smoothly on the water, and soon Darrell was reporting to me, "Tom has the message. They were at McAlister Lake like you said. The first message got hung up in the trees. The second one fell near their campsite." He shook his head. "I almost hit him with the third one."

I thanked him and Jim and was ready to go home. I couldn't do anything more till Tom came home. I got Amy and Sally, and we started home after agreeing to come back to have dinner with the Byrds.

As I pulled into our yard, I saw the garden. Then I remembered.

"Oh no!" I shouted. "I forgot and left the water running in the garden. The garden will be ruined! It only takes ten minutes to fill the trench, and I've been gone almost three hours."

As I ran to the garden, I was sure that I would find it completely flooded. All that work all spring would be wasted. There would be no fresh vegetables in just a few weeks, and none for the freezer for next winter.

When I got to the garden, I stopped, stunned at what I saw. It was not flooded. It was not ruined. The hose was still running, and the trench was full, but not one drop of water had overflowed.

"My God," I whispered, as I moved the hose to the next trench. "You've done this. You've kept this water from ruining the garden. You've taken this much care of Your garden. You've caused a miracle to happen just to save these vegetables. Why should I be worried about any of my problems? The Scriptures talk about Your care of the sparrow. Now I know that You take the same gentle care of all things that are Yours. Thank You, Father, that I am Yours also. Surely if You take this care of a garden, You will take care of me."

27

When I was on the road to the landing on my way to learn about Daddy's death, the Lord had promised me He would be with me. He kept His promise. That evening the Lord was with me in the form of a young man named Greg. Greg was working on a trail crew based in Stehekin. When the crew was in town, Greg came to our Bible studies. He was a friend of many of the summer employees at the lodge. Greg was a wonderful, caring Christian with a special gift for listening. The Lord brought him to me that first night I was without a father. Greg listened and nodded and smiled and blew his nose and made understanding comments far into the night. I shall never forget his kindness.

That evening my mind was filled with a collage of moments in my life with my daddy. I remembered how he took care of me when I was eight years old and had polio. I did not go to a hospital because there was an epidemic of polio at the time and the doctors felt I would be better off at home if my parents were willing to care for me. I was paralyzed completely except for my lungs. I could not even speak. I remember Daddy struggling into my room with Mother's wringer washing machine. Daddy had carried it all the way to the second floor from the basement. My treatment called for pieces of wool to be boiled for twenty minutes, then wrung out so that the water would not burn me, and then applied directly to my limbs and body. Even after struggling up two flights of stairs with that washing machine, Daddy smiled at me lying immobile in my bed.

"Thought if you're going to be in here all the time, you might as well do the washing for your mom," he joked.

I didn't understand what was happening until the first treatment, when I saw how the machine was to be used.

Mother boiled the wool pieces in the pot that fit into the cooking well at the back of her stove. Daddy carried the heavy deep-well pot upstairs from the kitchen to my bedroom. He fished out the steaming pieces of wool and ran them through the wringer twice. Then he tossed them to Mother, who pinned them on me. I cried. Mother cried. And Daddy stood quietly by the wringer.

Later two of the treatments each day were replaced by hot baths. Mother prepared the water while Daddy prepared me. He wrapped me in a sheet-blanket and picked me up to carry me into the bathroom. It always hurt terribly to be bent or moved. I was now able to talk, and I would cry out, "Please, Daddy, don't do that. It hurts me."

"I'm sorry, Lois," he would say with deep tenderness in his eyes. "I have to do it."

I would sob as he carried me down the hall, until one day I noticed that Daddy was biting his lip till it bled. I understood in that moment how much Daddy hurt, too. I also knew how much he loved me.

In the evenings Daddy would come into my room and read to me from his Bible. I didn't really understand what he read, but it didn't matter. I saw the comfort and support that Daddy got from the Bible. And that was enough.

My collage of memories jumped ahead to the time I was twelve. I was in the hospital having back surgery. The hospital was located in St. Petersburg, about four hours by the current roads from our home. I was in that hospital for eight months. The patients were allowed visitors only once a week, on Saturday afternoon. Despite the distance and time involved, my parents missed only one Saturday's visit in eight months. All the rooms had windows into the hall, and I remember lying in bed with my eyes fastened on the window on Saturday afternoon. Waiting, waiting. Then I would hear them, Mother's quick, light steps and Daddy's long, striding, heavy steps. Then I'd see them. They always stopped at the window and waved. There was Mother, small and lovely, smiling and crying at the same time. She always cried when she came. And there was Daddy, standing behind her, his chin nearly touching the top of her head. He'd come in first and pull my big toe and say, "Hi, Squirrelie!" Oh, how I loved them both!

There were so many things Daddy did for me to show how much he loved me. One summer he built a screened porch on the front of the house so that I could lie outside. Once when I was in a full body cast in the hospital, my family moved into a new house. I was allowed to come home for a few weeks, though it meant a great deal of work for my mother. I was excited to see the house all finished, as it was still being built when I went into the hospital. Even though I was twelve years old and in a full body cast, Daddy carried me through every room of the house so that I could see it. I remember how the veins stood out on his forehead while he carried me through the house.

Oh, and remember how proud he was the day I graduated from high school and got so many awards, both for service and for scholarship. Then there was the time he and Mother drove all the way from Florida to my college in Ohio to spend Dad's Day Weekend with me.

And how could I ever forget my wedding day? I was deeply in love with Tom. The whole family was. But it was hard to let go of Daddy's arm and take Tom's hand. The struggle ended when Daddy moved my hand from his arm and put it in Tom's keeping.

How I enjoyed watching Daddy play with my daughters the way he had played with my brother and sister and me. He made his incredible faces at them and hauled them around on his shoulders and teased them. He listened and dreamed and imagined with them as he had done with us.

Thank You, God, that You gave me this man to be my father.

28

About two o'clock the next afternoon, Dr. Bowles's truck stopped in front of the cabin, and Tom jumped out. Dr. Bowles had picked Tom up at the trail head and brought him home. The three girls and Edith were still on their way down the mountain, about an hour behind Tom.

The next few moments were ones of embracing and tears and sharing. We tried to decide what should be done and how it could be done. Finally it was time to pick the campers up. Tom had not showered yet, and he was hot and dirty from the eleven-mile hike. I offered to go to the trail head to get the girls.

They were waiting when I arrived. They looked at me quietly and seemed relieved when I smiled at them. "How was your trip? I'm sorry you had to come out a day early," I said.

They rushed at me, and I was lost in a tangle of loving arms. Isa poked a crumpled paper in my hand.

"It's a letter I wrote to you last night after we heard about your father. I knew I'd have trouble telling you what I want to say, so I wrote it down."

"Thank you, Isa."

But she wasn't finished. "Lois—" she faltered. "I—well—I want you to know that I—well, I prayed for you last night."

It was my turn to gulp. "Thank you, Isa. It really helped me, too. It wasn't too bad last night."

"Oh, I'm glad," she said as she flung her arms around me again.

Tom and I decided that we would have to stop the camping experience, even though it was barely half over. One girl had planned to stay nearby with friends after the camp. They agreed that she could come early. Another girl had a sister in Seattle, so we made arrangements to take her there when we went to Seattle for me to get the plane to Florida. Isa decided she'd just go back to Ohio now. We hoped that we could fly to Chicago together. Tom and our girls planned to drive to California to be with Tom's parents while I was in Florida. Everything was arranged. We packed quickly, and by five o'clock we were at the landing again to fly to Chelan and then drive on to Seattle.

But that wasn't the way the Lord planned it. Once more in our lives we were frustrated by the wind. Ernie could not fly because of the intensity of the wind. There was nothing to do but go back home. It was hard for me to take this final delay. It meant many more hours would pass before I could be with my family in Florida. The one encouraging thing was that a friend, Bill, offered to take us downlake early in the morning in his own boat. It was large enough to carry us all. We gratefully accepted his offer.

We went back home again, and I cooked dinner for all of us. The girls were very understanding and helpful. Isa picked a big bowl of peas, and another girl, Heidi, picked a salad and put it together. The third girl, Heather, helped me in the kitchen while my own daughters set the table. After dinner we had a very moving prayer time together. They shared about their trip and about how they'd felt when the plane dropped the message. They shared how they'd comforted Tom with Edith's help. We felt a very close relationship had been developed by the time we said good night.

By noon the next day we were stopping in front of the Seattle-Tacoma Airport. Tom helped me out and told me to go get in line while he got my bags and parked the truck.

"How will I buy the ticket, Tom?" I asked. "I don't have any money."

We had discussed this before and had not found an answer. Here it was time to buy the ticket, and I was still penniless.

"I don't know how we will pay for it. Just go get in line."

"Okay, Lord," I said. "Here goes. It's Your thing. You showed me You could take care of Your garden. Take care of me now."

There were four long lines at the United Airlines counter. I got in the longest and waited. Gradually I was getting closer to the front. What was I going to do when I got there? Could I get a ticket by just saying, "Excuse me, sir, but my father just died in Florida, and I'd like to go to his funeral. Will you give me a ticket, please?" I doubted that would get me onto the plane.

There was one more person before I would reach the counter. I was beginning to feel desperate. "Lord," I reminded him, "I'm counting on You to take care of this."

Just then I turned around and looked at the people in the line about four feet from mine. I noticed a very tall man with his back to me. He was second from the front in his line, too. As I looked at him, he turned and looked at me. It was Tom's sister's husband, Richard.

"Well! Hello!" he said. "Fancy meeting you here. You're not going to Orlando, are you?" he said with a knowing smile.

"Yes. How did you know?"

"Well, when Tom called us from Chelan to ask if he and Sally and Amy could stay with us for a couple of days and told us about your trip, he asked to borrow some money for a ticket. I thought it would be better for me to just get the ticket for you. So I came over and bought you one." He held it out and showed it to me. I started to take it. He pulled it back.

"Don't get excited. I'll check in for you."

I tried to tell him how grateful I was. I also told him I couldn't pay him back right now.

"So who cares?" he shrugged. "Do it when you can."

Later Isa and I sat together on our way to Chicago. We had four hours to think and talk together. Isa was another evidence that the Lord had not left me alone. We talked about Isa and her life, and we talked about me and mine. And we talked about God and how He worked in people's lives.

Isa finally shared this: "At first I thought what you were telling us these last two weeks was just talk. I didn't really believe it was real. I'm sorry that your daddy died, but I'm glad that I could be with you now. I've seen that what you've said is real. It's not just talk. You've shown me the last two days that God really does care and really does want a relationship with us. Remember when we talked by the river that night and I asked you what if I didn't like what God gave me? You said that maybe I wouldn't like it, but it would always be what was best for me. Remember that?"

I nodded.

"Well now I see what you meant. Sometimes what we get isn't the goodest, but it's the best. What you have been given right now doesn't taste good, but somehow God has it planned to be the best."

I looked into her clear, shining blue eyes. They were full of caring and understanding. I loved her.

About a month later we received a letter from Isa that she had accepted Jesus as her Savior and had joined a group of Christians. She had also started a noon-hour Bible study at her school. Praise God!

29

I stood beside the coffin and spoke in my thoughts to the man in it.

"You look like my daddy.

"You are wearing my daddy's suit.

"You are tanned like my daddy from working outdoors as a carpenter and playing golf every chance you get.

"You have white curly hair like my daddy. How pretty it is, too. Forgive me for always regretting my hair was curly like yours. I guess it really is pretty. I guess I should thank my daddy for giving me curly hair.

"Sir, I can't see your eyes. Are they blue and sparkling like my daddy's? Do they reach out with love and forgiveness like my daddy's? Can they reprimand louder and more completely than ten spankings?

"I see the little crow's-feet beside your eyes. Daddy had those. He never liked to wear sunglasses. He just squinted instead.

"Your mouth doesn't look like my daddy's. He smiled at me or made funny faces with his mouth.

"But your hands. They almost convince me that you are Daddy. I can't look at them. I don't want it to be you, Daddy."

I turned away and talked with my sister. She was very broken. Daddy had been very special to her, too. Sara was concerned that I had not cried. "You need to cry, Lois. Don't keep holding it in. You must let it out."

"I don't have any tears, Sara. Why should I be sad? Daddy

loved the Lord. He's with Jesus now. Just think of all the glory he's in now. How can I cry about that?"

"I know that, too," she said. "That's the only thing that keeps me from going under completely. But I loved Daddy so. How can I give him up?" She began to cry again. "Who will help me like he did? Nobody. Oh, Daddy, I need you!"

She began to sob again and stroke Daddy's hair. I turned away and talked with an old friend from high school days. I enjoyed seeing him again. Many other people came. The evening passed, and the night. The next morning I was standing at the coffin again. It would be the last time before the lid would be closed and it would be taken into the chapel for the services later in the morning.

I stood holding onto Mother as she sobbed quietly, "I know he's with You, Lord. And I praise You for that. But did You need to take him so soon? He's so young. Couldn't I have had him a little longer?"

The strain of the last few days was beginning to accumulate. I was feeling it. And I hated to see my family so upset. It was all beginning to sink in.

I had come a long way—by water, by car, by plane. It had all seemed rather like a dream, unreal somehow. I had been numb, but now the numbness was beginning to wear off.

Mother stopped crying. We still had our arms around each other, but now she was supporting me. I was looking at his hands. In my mind I spoke to them.

"You are so beautiful. So strong. So tanned. Think of all the lovely things you have made—chairs and tables with carved legs, candlesticks and fruit bowls. Do you remember the rolling pin at home in my kitchen? You made it for me from a limb of the maple tree. And think of the houses you've built for us and for other people. Remember the cabinets you built using only dowels and glue and no nails? I remember when I was a little girl I loved to stand next to you and watch you work. I wanted to laugh because the sawdust always got caught in your curly hair, even the hair on your fingers. Remember how you handed me the long curls that magically appeared from behind the plane when you pushed it across a piece of wood? I loved those curls. I put them in my hair and pretended I was a blonde fairy queen.

"Remember how warm you always were? I loved to have you reach out and grab me and throw me in the air or just squeeze me close to your body. I liked it, too, when you would tousle my hair or tickle my feet. And remember all those times you carried me.

"Oh I want to touch you.

"I want to feel your warmth. I want to feel you squeeze me again.

"Oh but I know you won't. You're dead. You're not really my daddy anymore. Just his body."

But still—

"Go ahead and touch him, Lois," my mother encouraged me. "It will be good for you to understand."

She spoke so quietly and so strongly. I looked at her. She was very calm.

"You're all right, aren't you, Mother?"

"Yes I am. The Spirit is helping me. Go ahead, Lois. Cry."

I saw that indeed my mother was being helped by the Spirit.

"I was afraid to cry, to break down, if you needed me to be strong," I sobbed on her shoulder. "I was afraid you needed me to be strong."

"I do. But not right now. Later. Go ahead and grieve for your daddy."

A dam inside of me broke. I hung with one hand onto my mother's shoulder and with the other held the cold, lifeless hand of my father and released myself to grief.

But I did not go under. I was not consumed as I had been afraid that I would be. There was under me a strong support that would not give way. Even as I sobbed with my broken heart, a picture flashed through my mind. It was a picture of my garden. It was just as I had left it, nearly ready to harvest. Wild animals stood around the edges but did not eat from it. Just the right amount of water flowed in the trenches, not one drop too much. God was taking perfect care of it. I heard Him say to me, "I take perfect care of what is Mine. You see I have allowed no harm to come to this garden. I will allow no harm to come to you. I have allowed no harm to come to your daddy. You are both in My care."

"Thank You, Father!"

For the remainder of the time of the funeral, I was at peace. I had not denied my feelings; they had been expressed, and God could now begin to heal them. Now I could truly be a help to others. I was busy witnessing my confidence in the Lord through actions because I sincerely knew His power and care.

I stayed with Mother for three weeks. It was a beautiful time of sharing, and I was able to help her begin to receive God's healing. She helped me, too, as I continued to work through the grief process. There were moments when I would be stabbed anew with the realization I would not see my father again on this earth. I treasured our times together, especially the summer they visited us in Stehekin. For weeks, and indeed even to this very day, there are moments I grieve for my father and yearn for his presence and touch. But our God is a faithful God, and just as He did not leave me when I first grieved, He does not leave me in my loss now.

Praise His Holy Name. He is our *rock* as well as our salvation.

30

"I've been thinking," Tom said. "What if—"

He stopped talking and seemed to focus his attention on the red and white bobber floating contentedly on top of the water. We were in our small fishing boat on the lake. How relaxing it was to sit in the warm August sun and be gently rocked by the waves. The girls were on an expedition with Edith, so Tom and I had the day to ourselves. I sat down on the floor of the boat and leaned back against a seat cushion. I looked up at Tom.

What a change had come over this man in the last year. He was still incredibly handsome, especially at this time of year, when he was tanned from being outside all the time. His dark hair accentuated his darkened skin. Our years in the wilderness had added to the girth of his shoulders and upper arms. His hands were strong, and the skin was toughened in several places on the palms. I smiled to think of that first fall when he had to cut wood for the first time. His hands were not used to such work. Before the wood was gathered they had actually swelled to twice their normal size. But now look at them. I watched as they gently pulled on the fishing line teasing some unsuspecting fish in the depths of the lake.

But it wasn't just his physical self that had changed. There was a new confidence about him, confidence in himself, and yet the source of the confidence was not in himself; it was his new relationship with the Lord. Together they were making a new man.

He turned his attention back to the conversation. He took off his sunglasses and looked carefully at me.

"What do you think about me going into the ministry?"

I smiled. "Well, it depends on why you want to, I guess."

"God is calling me into the ministry. I really believe it. For months now, every time I begin to pray, this great conviction fills my mind, 'I want you in the ministry.' It's a crazy idea as far as I'm concerned."

"Why?"

"Well, just for beginners, I'd probably have to go to seminary. How could I do that? I have a family to support. I can't just go off to school for a few years. And besides that I'm almost thirty-seven years old. That's kinda late to start a new profession. Anyway I like teaching. Seems like I could work for the Lord and still stay in my profession."

"Yes you could, but it wouldn't work if the Lord wanted you to do something else. And what's wrong with being thirty-seven? Think how old Moses was when God called him to stop trailing after sheep and start leading people. And as far as worrying about your family, that's touching and all, but who really is our source? Don't use us to keep from doing what God is calling you to do."

He grinned and looked at the bobber again. "I should have known you'd be on God's side."

Just then the bobber disappeared, and there was a jerk on the line. Tom pulled sharply on the pole and began reeling in the line. I sat up straight to watch the action. We'd caught hundreds of fish from this lake, but it was still thrilling to hook into one, especially if it was a trout. Tom got this one up to the boat and scooped the net under it. It was one of the beautiful silver salmon that were so bountiful in the lake. It shimmered in the sun as it flopped and jerked at the end of the line.

"Thank You, Jesus," Tom said. "That's fifteen this morning. With the ten at home, we need only five more and we can do a batch in the smoker. Thank You, Lord, for providing for our needs."

He put the fish on the stringer and lowered it over the side of the boat. I leaned back again and watched him slip another worm onto the hook. The mountains rose sharply in the distance behind him. They were covered with pine and fir and maple. Here and there were clumps of wild flowers.

"What would it be like to be a minister's wife?" I thought. First of all it would mean leaving here. Something tightened inside me.

"I don't even know how to begin to go into the ministry." Tom returned to his subject as he tossed the worm into the water and began to let out line.

"Bruce will be coming up to the services this weekend. You could ask him," I suggested.

"Um-huh, I could." He seemed to be talking to his bobber again.

For the rest of the week we did not talk of it again. As a matter of fact Tom didn't really talk much at all. He had been walking a lot since I'd returned from Florida, but now he was gone, wandering the trails for two or three hours a day, or he fished alone. When he was at home, he was deep in thought. I watched him work mechanically in the garden. He seldom played with the girls, and then it was in a rather noninvolved way, such as pushing them on the rope swing. I noticed him sitting on the ground, leaning against a stump beside the smoker.

"Tom, there's not much smoke coming out of the side there," I said.

"What? Oh!" He threw down the blade of grass he'd been chewing on and got the smoke going again.

As I watched, I prayed, "Lord, let Your will be done. If You really are calling him into the ministry, it would be a tremendous change in our lives. But if that's what You want, make us willing to be willing."

Saturday night Tom and Bruce and I were sitting in our cabin living room. Tom and Bruce were on the couch, discussing various aspects of the new church. Then the conversation lagged. Tom looked at me and took a deep breath.

"Help him, Jesus," I prayed silently.

He turned to face Bruce and said very simply, "The Lord is calling me into the ministry. How do I do it?"

It was as though an electric shock had gone through Bruce. He sat up erect and looked at Tom and then at me and back to Tom. Joy began to spread over his face, and tears came to his eyes. He reached over and gripped Tom's knee.

"I think that's wonderful!" He looked at me again. My smile showed my willingness. "Just wonderful!" he repeated.

He leaned back again, and in the next minutes he began to tell us how one entered the ministry in the United Methodist Church. It sounded like a long process, one that could not be accomplished on a whim. Yes, among other things, it did mean schooling—three to four years. Bruce promised to make the necessary contacts for Tom to get the process started. He said he would also arrange for the district superintendent to come up to Stehekin on a weekend preaching mission. Then we could talk with him and get all the details.

Early that fall Norm and his family came, and we had a lovely weekend with them. Norm asked many questions, some of which were very hard to answer. After all, Tom and I were really very ignorant of many things pertaining to the church. We hadn't even been in a church for over three years. We had no idea how they functioned. All we knew was that we'd had a life-transforming experience with the Lord, one that was growing into a beautiful relationship with Him. That's all we knew. We were innocents, literally babes in the woods. We admitted it. Norm was very helpful and supportive. When he left, he promised to send us catalogs of seminaries where Tom might like to go.

They arrived, and after much debate and prayer we chose one. We felt sure it was the Lord's leading. It was in Denver, Colorado. Tom filled in the application with this prayer, "Lord, this all still seems a little crazy to me, but I'm sure You've called me to do it. I don't see how it will work out, but I'm leaving that to You. If it is Your doing, You'll have to make it happen. Lord, I'm trying to trust and obey. If this really is what You want, for me to go through seminary and all that, then You have them accept me. There are plenty of reasons why they might not, my age or whatever. But, Lord, this is the only place I'm going to apply. I'm going to put out one last fleece like Gideon did. If You really want me in the professional ministry, have this school accept me. Amen."

He dropped the letter into the mailbag with some other outgoing mail and drove to the landing. When he returned, he came out to the garden where I was cutting the last of the cabbage.

"Well it's done," he announced.

"I'm glad," I said. "Now that it is, there's something I want to tell you. I didn't want to tell you before because I didn't want it to influence your decision. I wanted it to be a confirmation for you. Something happened to me years ago that I never told you. I didn't understand it then, but I do now." And I shared with him the vision that I'd had of him as a minister back in Ohio years before.

When I finished telling him, he took me in his arms, and we stood there embracing in the cabbage patch behind a cabin deep in a wilderness in the mountains. We both realized at that moment that we had a future neither of us would ever have thought of even in our wildest imagination.

31

Late October means one thing in the wilderness: hunting season. The tourists were long gone, but we now received an influx of hunters. But at the same moment the hunters arrived, the deer vanished. They truly had to be hunted.

I felt a little uneasy when I saw all the hunters wandering along the road. I had even heard them in the woods behind our cabin one day when I was hanging laundry out. I hoped they realized I was not a deer spelled with two e's.

Richard always came for a few days, and we enjoyed his stay very much. He got in a lot of walking. Tom went with him after school, too. They walked all over the area. But we always waved Richard good-bye without his taking a hunk of venison home with him. He left a gun for Tom, and Tom continued to hope he would use it. But he never did. A couple of grouse were all the wild game we'd eaten the whole time we were here.

But this fall Tom had an added incentive. We were running out of meat, and we didn't really have the money to buy more. The last day of hunting season arrived, and Tom had kept his old record of not even seeing a buck. This was his last day to find one.

The weather was helpful this year. It had snowed in the high country in the last few days. That would drive the game down to lower altitudes. There was a trail that the deer used near High Bridge, up past the Courtney place. He decided to try there.

Before sunup that last hunting day, Tom was on his way. About two hours later he was back home. One look at his face and I knew he'd gotten a buck. I had expected all those days he went hunting to see him come home with a big smile of triumph the day he had been successful. But how wrong I was. He looked terrible. He looked an awful color somewhere between green and gray.

I met him at the door.

"I got one," he said flatly.

"Where is it?"

"In the back of the car." He went past me toward the bathroom.

"Are you all right?" I asked.

"Yes, but it was terrible! I'm going to wash my hands."

I walked out to the car. One look and I understood. It was a good-sized deer with three points on its antlers. There were several bullet holes in its head, and its throat was cut. Its abdomen had also been opened and emptied. No wonder Tom was sick. He could hardly stand to kill the rabbits Sally had raised for meat. Sally hadn't minded the rabbits being killed, although she didn't watch. But Tom said he'd never do it again. Sally kept the mother rabbit as a pet for a while, and then Frank, one of our valley friends, took it to raise more rabbits.

Tom came out about the time Frank was driving by to church. He helped Tom drag the animal out of the car (what a job it must have been to get it in alone!), and they hung it by the back legs from a big branch of the maple tree in front of the cabin. Frank showed Tom how to skin the deer. I decided I didn't want to drive the bloody car to church, so the girls and I rode with Frank and his family.

When we got home, Tom had just completed the skinning. The head had also been removed. I helped him draw a game bag made of muslin over the carcass to keep the insects off of it. We planned to let it hang from the tree for a few days to let it age and become more tender.

After Tom had showered and had a bite of lunch, he told us what had happened.

"I told the Lord that if I'd ever get a deer, He'd have to show it to me and it would have to be close enough for me to hit it. I'd never shot this rifle, and besides it was a 30-30, not exactly a deer gun. As I approached the Courtney's place, the sun was not up, so it was still dark. I thought I saw some animals moving around in the field. Because of the darkness, I wasn't sure if they were deer or horses. I took the rifle and crept into the field. I went over a little hill, and as I looked down, I saw four young deer looking back at me. Two continued to look at me, and the other two went back to grazing. I thought I had so quietly sneaked up on them, but they'd known I was there before I knew they were there. Since they were does, I went back to the car.

"As I started up the road toward High Bridge, snow began to fall. By the time I went up the last steep grade, there was enough light that I could see clearly for a short distance. I felt confident because it seemed these were perfect conditions—barely light, cold, and snowing. Just as I came over the rise, I saw two bucks standing in the middle of the bridge about twenty-five yards away. One was so large I thought for a moment it was an elk. They saw me the same time I saw them. I stopped the car, and we looked at each other.

" 'Come on deer. Come on over to this side of the bridge where you're not protected by the game preserve,' I whispered to them.

"In an instant they turned and vanished back into the protected area. I began to chuckle. 'Lord, You're really teasing me!' Still it seemed obvious that the deer were moving, so I parked the car. As the deer came down from the high country, they would be coming right past here.

"It was so cold I stayed in the car, but I got in the back seat where I'd have more room. I was watching the bridge, and my back was to the trail to Coon Lake. I sat there for about fifteen minutes. Suddenly I felt I should turn around and look behind me. I turned, and there was a three-point buck standing about ten yards away.

" 'Wow!' I thought. I reached for the rifle. The deer continued to browse, moving slowly away from the car and toward the trail. I slid the back window open and stuck the rifle out the window. I aimed at his head because I wanted to preserve the meat. I pulled the trigger, and the noise rang through the car like a cannon. The deer never moved. I didn't hit it, but still it failed to move. He seemed confused about where the noise came from. Then the deer began to walk slowly, heading toward the shed that was used by the rangers during the summer. When the deer went behind the shed, I climbed out of the car. When the deer came into view on the other side of the shed, I shot at it again. I hit it in the head this time. He jumped off the ground and then ran behind the shed and toward the trail.

"I ran to where the deer had been, and I saw blood in the snow. Suddenly I realized that if I didn't find him and kill him, he would just wander off in the woods and die. It was easy to track him because there were drops of blood periodically in the fresh snow. I went up the trail a short way, but I didn't see the deer. Suddenly he jumped up off the slope ahead of me. He started to run, and I shot again. I hit him the second time in the head. He fell. I started toward him, and he tried to jump up again.

"I felt sick. This poor animal! I was sorry I'd started the whole thing. I wished it would die and be out of its agony. With my insides churning, I shot him in the head again, and he fell silent.

"He was lying on a hill, so I turned him head down and slit his throat to bleed him. As the red blood began to stain the white snow, I began to sweat. It was very cold out, but I was hot and nauseated. I remember thanking the Lord for the deer, but I wasn't sure anymore that I wanted it.

"After it was bled, I drug it down the trail. Then I realized I would have to field-dress it. I didn't really know how. I was afraid to cut too deeply for fear of hitting the entrails.

" 'Lord,' I said. 'I need help. I don't know how to do this.'

"At that moment I heard a motor, and thinking maybe some hunters were coming up the road, I ran down the trail toward the road, and there, to my joy, were four hunters getting out of a truck.

" 'I got one, and I need help,' I shouted to them. 'I don't know how deep to cut.'

"One of the men came back up the trail with me and made the first cut. After telling me how to finish it, he left. I continued to work and I thanked the Lord for sending the man. Then I realized my hands were very cold and sticky. I thought, 'Lord, if I had to kill all our meat, I'm afraid we'd be vegetarians!'

"I cleaned out the cavity, put the liver aside for a meal, buried the entrails under a rock, and began to drag the deer to the car. I was amazed to discover how heavy it was. 'Thank You, Lord, that I didn't get a deer in the high country, where I was hunting before. I never would have gotten it out! I guess You knew that, didn't You?'

"'How am I going to get it in the car?' I wondered. The men were gone. When I tried to get one end of the deer in the back of the car, the other end would just roll around. It must have been comical to see. That deer was like a huge, very heavy roll of jelly. When it was finally in the car, I was exhausted. I leaned against the door to talk to Jesus.

"'Thank You, Lord, for that deer. I didn't think it would be like this. I guess I didn't really know what I was asking for. I feel sick.'"

The weather was perfect for aging the meat. The temperature stayed between thirty-eight and forty-three degrees for eight days. We could tell by poking the flanks that it was becoming tender. We had already eaten the liver, and it was delicious, even though we are not a liver-loving family. We were looking forward to tasting the meat.

On the eighth day Frank came by to show us how to cut it up. We had borrowed the Courtney's cleaver and heavy knives, and we were ready to work. And work it was! We hacked off a quarter and carried it inside. We had covered the table with a heavy piece of lumber and plastic. Tom wielded the cleaver, and I cut smaller pieces. Then I wrapped it in freezer wrap, and the girls marked it. It was the messiest job I'd ever done. Hours later, when we finished, we were exhausted, and the kitchen was a mess. It was days before I could forget that slippery feeling of the meat in my hands and that strong odor of fresh venison. It was three weeks before we brought any of it out of the freezer to eat. Then we were sorry we had waited so long. It was absolutely delicious! It was not strong-tasting at all. I had expected a gamy flavor. It did have a distinct flavor, but it was not a strong one. And it was tender enough that we could cut it with a fork. The venison steaks were better than any meat I've ever eaten, without a doubt. But what an experience we'd had getting it! We felt sure we would not want to do it again. Maybe we weren't the wilderness people we'd thought we were after all.

32

It was November. I was at the boat dock, waving good-bye to Tom. He was headed for a retreat in Wenatchee that was being led by a professor from the seminary where Tom had applied. It seemed strange to us that Tom was leaving the woods to go to a retreat in the city. But it was only for a weekend, and I guess the participants didn't have time to go away somewhere. Tom planned to be a somewhat silent observer of the whole thing.

Just minutes before, Randi had stepped off the boat for a weekend in Stehekin. She was our friend who had worked at the lodge that summer. She was now living and studying at Holden Village, which was a Christian retreat in our area. Randi had come to spend the weekend with the girls and me. We were very excited to have her.

Late into the night Randi and I talked and shared what the Lord was doing in our lives. However, I did not mention Tom's new decision. We had told no one outside of Bruce and Norm. What I did share with Randi was something that was lying very heavily on my heart. My mother.

I had always had a close relationship with my mother. I'd had surgery seven times, and she had struggled with me through every one of them. She had spent hours every day manipulating my limbs to help the muscles regain their function. She had supported me in everything I'd ever done, and now that she was alone, I felt a great need to support her. I grieved for her loneliness. I cried over every letter she wrote us. I was deeply frustrated because I could not help her. I wrote to her often. The girls and

Tom and I made cassette tapes for her. The girls made pictures for her. We all prayed constantly for her. But all these things seemed to me to be very inadequate. What she needed, I thought, was someone to be with her, someone to cheer her up, help her keep her house, cook for her, help her keep the car in good repair. I couldn't do any of those things. I was thousands of miles away. I couldn't even talk to her on a phone.

I had wanted to bring her home with me that summer, but we finally decided it would be too hard for her to go back home to an empty house. We also thought it would be good for her to have something to look forward to in coming to visit us. We had decided Christmas would be a good time for her to come, but she had recently written us a letter saying she could not come. Her financial situation was not good, and she simply did not have the money for a plane ticket. I was more than disappointed; I began to be depressed about it. I shared all this with Randi.

"I don't understand it, Randi. Why doesn't the Lord help us to be together? What is a plane ticket to Him? It seems to me to be a very little thing compared to the big things He's done for us. Why Randi? Why can't I be with my mother?" I was crying by this time.

We were sitting on the floor in front of the fire. The house was very quiet. I heard one of the girls turning in her sleep. A coyote howled somewhere on a distant bluff.

Randi put down the sock she was knitting.

"I don't know the answer, Lois. But maybe—" She stopped while I blew my nose. "Maybe it's best this way. If you were with your mother, she would be depending on you. This way she has to learn to depend on the Lord. And so do you," she added very quietly.

I knew she was right. She was absolutely right. Once more I was seeing that the best is not always the "goodest."

We prayed together and went to bed.

Next morning, after a festive breakfast of Swedish *äggkaka* that Randi made for us, she announced, "I'd like to borrow your car for a few minutes. I want to go to the restaurant and get a few things. Tonight I'm going to cook a special dinner for you. Lois, I want you to get lost today. Go do whatever you want, visit somebody, take a hike, whatever. Just disappear."

"Gosh! I'm being ordered away from my own house."

"Exactly! Now scram!"

"What about Sally and Amy?"

"They stay. They're in on this, too. Now, shoo!" She flapped the dishtowel at me.

About four o'clock I crept up to the side door.

"Randi," I called quietly, almost afraid for her to know I was back. "Randi, it'll be dark soon. Can I come in?"

"Okay, but close your eyes, and we'll lead you into your room. You have to stay there until we say you can come out."

For the next hour and a half, I heard giggling and scurrying feet and pots and pans rattling. Fantastic aromas floated in under my door. Then I heard the girls in their room whispering. I even heard a bath being run in the tub. My curiosity was killing me. I tried to read to keep my mind off what was going on in my house.

At last the bedroom door opened. I was greeted by my two daughters, scrubbed till they shone and dressed in their very best long dresses. Their hair was tied up in ribbons. Their eyes sparkled.

"Okay, Mommy. Come see what we have for you."

I followed them into the darkened living room. I gasped at the beautiful sight.

The maple kitchen table and chairs had been moved into the living room in front of the open fireplace. On the table were our best blue linen placemats and napkins. Dried wild flowers sat in the center of the table between two lit candles. The flowers were reflected in the crystal goblets. Our white china with tiny blue flower trim completed this breathtaking sight. The whole scene was reflected again and again in the dark windows. The elegance was spectacular. We had not used any of these things since we came to the wilderness. Somehow I had mistakenly thought they didn't fit. I had forgotten their beauty. But more than the elegance, the act of true love and caring radiated in the dark night.

All I could say was, "Oh girls! It's so beautiful. Thank you."

"Go sit down, Mama," Sally instructed me. "I'll bring you the first course."

I started toward the table and saw my reflection in the windows.

"Could you wait just one minute? Would it ruin anything if I just ran into my room for a minute?" I asked.

"Okay, but hurry, Mommy."

I dashed into the bedroom and came out three minutes later.

"Wow, Mommy, you look pretty," the girls squealed.

I had changed into my best long dress and had fixed my hair, too. With true elegance I took my daughters' arms and said, "Will you ladies seat me at my table, please?"

What an elegant evening it was! What exquisite people we were! What elaborate and delicious food we ate! Each time we glanced at the window reflection, we were sure we were in an enchanted forest. And just maybe we were!

33

Once more there was a laden tree inside the cabin. Banners hung all around. The crèches were out, and enticing presents lay begging to be opened. It was Christmas Eve. Edith was with us for a special Christmas Eve dinner and celebration. Tomorrow we would eat with her and the Byrd family in the closed restaurant.

At bedtime Sally and Amy hung their stockings near the fire and galloped off to bed in their heavy "fuzzies" (their name for their winter pajamas).

Santa did his age-old thing once more, and morning found two children deep in the woods, squealing over their gifts.

Part of the fun and excitement was missing for me. I had so looked forward to sharing this Christmas with my mother. Now I was missing her so much, and yes I missed Daddy, too. Somehow there was a hole in this celebration. With little excitement I watched the children unwrap their gifts. I was not anxious to open mine.

Sally handed me a box that I'd seen Edith carry in the night before. "It's probably one of those pretty vases she's been making," I thought. I opened it and found I was right. But there was something else in the box. An envelope. I opened it, and a piece of paper fell out. When I picked it up off the floor, I saw that it was a check made out to me in the amount of four hundred dollars. At the bottom left was written, "For a plane ticket for Nanny."

I stared at it, trying to comprehend what I saw. Then it hit me. Here was the money we'd all been praying for to get my mother out here to see us. From that moment on the day had a completely different look.

We drove immediately to the landing. Edith was bustling around the kitchen of the restaurant, cooking the Christmas dinner for all of us. I ran to her and flung my arms around her. I couldn't speak. All I could do was cry.

"Every time I ate with you," Edith was explaining between her own sniffing, "I'd hear Amy and Sally praying for money for Nanny to get a plane ticket. When I put them to bed, they would pray again for it. The Lord began to work on me. He wanted me to give you the money. I have to admit I wasn't very willing at first, but finally He got to me, and so did the kids. I'm glad I did it. It's one of the most fun things I've ever done."

"Sometimes it's hard to do what the Lord wants," Tom said. "But it's exciting, too." Then he added very quietly, "I know!"

The day after Christmas we found a letter from Denver in our mailbox. The seminary had accepted Tom.

34

"Hey, Tom, listen to this," I said. We were sitting at the table one evening shortly after Christmas. I was reading my Bible, and Tom was poring over our family finances. He looked up as I read to him from Psalm 34.

> O taste and see that the Lord is good: blessed is the man that trusteth in him. O fear the Lord, ye his saints: for there is no want to them that fear him. The young lions do lack, and suffer hunger: but they that seek the Lord shall not want any good thing. (8-10)

I turned the page and read from Psalm 36.

> How excellent is thy lovingkindness, O God! therefore, the children of men put their trust under the shadow of thy wings. They shall be abundantly satisfied with the fatness of thy house; and thou shalt make them drink of the river of thy pleasures. (7-8)

A cross-reference brought me to Psalm 84.

> For the Lord God is a sun and shield: the Lord will give grace and glory: no good thing will be withheld from them that walk uprightly. O Lord of hosts, blessed is the man that trusteth in thee. (11-12)

"Sounds pretty convincing, doesn't it?" Tom admitted. "It's true He has begun to provide for us. That grant from the seminary for the first quarter's tuition is a big help. And since I finally started listening to the Lord about tithing, our bills are getting paid. Still

—we have to have something to live on the next few years till I'm through with school."

"That's true. But Amy is in school now, so I'll be able to work. If you have a part-time job, too, we should be able to make it," I said.

"Yes, but we have some more bills that need to be paid off first, and it won't be cheap moving."

Part of the answer came the next day. I was unexpectedly offered a job at the lodge. Bob Byrd's daughter, Annette, had been taking care of most of the office work. She had decided to take another job downlake and would be leaving right after the first of the year. Bob offered me the job. I took it!

It was strange to be working full time again, but it worked out very well. Sally and Amy were with Tom all day at school and went home with him. I finished work about four o'clock. Later, in the summer, when there was a great deal of business and I had taken over the majority of the office work, I very frequently worked ten hours a day. But an exciting thing was happening. As Tom kept on tithing and I worked, all our bills were paid. A savings account began to grow. Before we arrived at the seminary, we had three thousand dollars in the savings. Incredible! We had no idea where it all came from.

Tom filled out numerous applications for part-time work in the Denver area. He sent the applications to the seminary, and they forwarded the information to prospective employers. Some of the positions sounded exciting. Most were for part-time Christian education directors in churches or counselors at high schools or small colleges in the area. Tom qualified for them because of his master's degree in counseling. Some of the jobs offered more pay part time than Tom was getting full time right then.

In May the long-awaited visit from "Nanny" materialized. We had a delightful time together. How happy I was to see her! She looked older than I'd remembered, and she was still occasionally fighting her gallbladder problem, but she was the same "ol' sweet Nanny" we loved.

Because the lodge office work was entirely my responsibility, I could not take a complete vacation while Mother was with us. I had to work two or three hours a day just to take care of the immediate things. I stayed home with Mother until after the girls got home from school. She was delighted to spend time with them while I worked. One afternoon I was busy at the typewriter when a call came over the radio. I answered it and found that it was a man in Nebraska calling to talk to Tom. I explained, as I always did, that this was not an ordinary telephone, that it was really a radio on our end. I said that I could give a message to Mr. Olson, who, in fact, was my husband. The man introduced himself as Dick Carter and explained that he was a district superintendent of the United Methodist Church in Nebraska. He had seen some papers on Tom, and he would like to talk with him. We arranged to have Tom return his call the next afternoon at three-thirty. I couldn't wait to get home and tell him.

His reaction was, "Nebraska! I don't know any ministers in Nebraska! What does he want to talk to me about?"

"I don't know," I shrugged. "You'll find out tomorrow."

At three twenty-nine the call was going through.

"Hello, Dick Carter speaking."

Click.

"Hello, Mr. Carter. This is Lois Olson calling from Stehekin, Washington. I am the radio operator here. Tom Olson is standing by. A speaker is connected so that he can hear your conversation. I will relay what he says to you."

Click.

"Oh—well, I want to talk to him personally."

Click.

"I'm sorry, sir. It isn't possible. I will tell you exactly what he says."

Click.

"No, I insist on speaking to him personally."

Click.

"What should I do, Tom? He really wants to talk with you directly. Oh, phooey! Why not! Here. This is how you work the thing."

Click.

"One moment, please, Mr. Carter. Tom will be right with you."

Click.

"Good evening, sir. This is Tom Olson."

Click.

"Hello, Tom. I'm Dick Carter. I'm the superintendent of the Northwest District of the United Methodist Church in Nebraska. I was down at the seminary in Denver yesterday, and I got some paper work on you. I was very impressed. I'm looking for a pastor for a two-point charge in northwestern Nebraska, and I wondered if you would be interested."

"Nebraska!" Tom almost shouted.

"You have to push the thing, Tom, or he can't hear you," I said quickly.

"Oh yeah." He pushed it. "Nebraska!"

Click.

"Yes, Nebraska."

Click.

"Well, I'm pleased that you found my qualifications interesting, but I'll be going to school in Denver"—the secret was out now! All over the countryside!—"and that's in Colorado. Unless my geography is way off, Nebraska is quite a distance from Colorado. I couldn't possibly work in Nebraska."

Click.

"These little towns are on the western edge of the state, right at the Wyoming border. It would only be about two hundred miles one way."

"Two hundred miles!"

"The button, Tom."

Click.

"Two hundred miles?"

Click.

"Sure. Lots of fellas drive that far and farther. We have one student pastor who drives four hundred miles to his parish."

Click.

There was silence at both ends. Tom was stunned.

"Are you still there, Tom?"

Click.

"Ah yes, sir. I'm here. But, sir, even if I would drive"—Tom gulped—"two hundred miles one way, I have no idea how to be a pastor. I haven't set foot in a seminary yet."

Click.

"I know that."

Click.

"Why, I haven't even been in a church for almost four years. I wouldn't even know the order of worship!"

Click.

"Oh, that's no problem. The order of worship is printed in the front of the hymnal."

Tom's eyes bulged as he looked at me.

"I'd be glad to hel—" His voice was cut off because in the excitement Tom had pressed the button.

"Tom!" I whispered. "The button!"

"Oh yeah!"

"—and the churches are small—memberships of about eighty and a hundred thirty. They're only eight miles apart. The parsonage is located next to the Henry Church. It's a nice three-bedroom house—carpet and drapes and appliances."

He was beginning to sound like a real estate salesman!

"Your salary would be sixty-two hundred dollars per year. It would be good experience for you, too. What do you say, Tom?"

Click.

Tom couldn't say anything.

"Are you there, Tom?"

Click.

"Yes, I'm here." He said it very quietly.

Click.

"Well, what about it? Would you like the job?"

Click.

"Well, look, Mr. Carter. I'll have to think and pray about this for a while. I'll—ah—well—it isn't what I'd had in mind as a job. Being a pastor before I even go to seminary!"

Click.

"Okay. Well, I'll be out of town for the rest of the week. Why don't you give me a call late Sunday night, say about ten o'clock.

I'll be looking forward to hearing what you decide. Good night, Tom. It's been nice talking with you."

Click.

"Good night, sir. God bless you."

Click.

"Thank you, and you, too. Good-bye."

Click.

There was only the sound of the dial tone now.

Tom leaned back in the chair with a thump. "It's incredible! Me, a minister before I even go to school to learn how to be one! It's preposterous! And to drive two hundred miles *one* way. It's out of the question!"

"Oh I don't know," I said thoughtfully. "I think it would be kind of—interesting."

"You would!"

Tom did a lot of walking and praying that week. We both read a lot of Scripture, too. We were really seeking the Lord's will. Three things during that week were outstanding.

The first thing was that Tom kept telling me how he couldn't speak in front of a group of adults. Kids were one thing; adults were something else. And he had no idea whatsoever how to prepare a sermon. At the time I was taking a correspondence course from Moody Bible Institute in Chicago covering the Old Testament. I ran across the incident of God calling Moses. It seemed extremely appropriate.

"Here, Tom. Read this. Maybe it will help you."

> And Moses said unto the Lord, O my Lord, I am not eloquent, neither heretofore, nor since thou hast spoken unto thy servant: but I am slow of speech, and of a slow tongue. And the Lord said unto him, Who hath made man's mouth? or who maketh the dumb, or deaf, or the seeing, or the blind? have not I, the Lord? Now therefore go, and I will be with thy mouth, and teach thee what thou shalt say. (Exod. 4:10-12)

The second thing that happened was that all the applications Tom had sent out came back saying thanks for applying, we were impressed with your qualifications, but we've chosen someone else.

"I don't understand!" Tom cried. "I could do any of those jobs and do them well. I've been trained to do them. Why didn't I get one? Why have I been offered a job that I have no idea in the world how to do? Why, if I took that job as a pastor for two churches, I'd need the Lord every single second!"

"Exactly," the Lord said to him. "Exactly. You *will* need Me. You could do any of those other jobs, and you would take all the credit and give Me none. You wouldn't know that you must rely on Me constantly."

The third thing was another Scripture I found in Numbers 22. It was the story of Balaam and his ass. Balaam, hired by the enemy, was off to curse God's people and God was seeking to prevent Balaam from going. An angel kept appearing to the ass, frightening it so that it would lie down and not move forward. After the third time Balaam was in a rage. He struck the ass with his staff.

> And the Lord opened the mouth of the ass, and she said unto Balaam, What have I done unto thee, that thou hast smitten me three times? And Balaam said unto the ass, Because thou has mocked me: I would there were a sword in mine hand, for now would I kill thee. And the ass said unto Balaam, Am not I thine ass, upon which thou hast ridden ever since I was thine unto this day? was I ever wont to do so unto thee? And he said, Nay. Then the Lord opened the eyes of Balaam, and he saw the angel of the Lord standing in the way, and his sword drawn in his hand: and he bowed down his head, and fell flat on his face. (Num. 22:28-31)

"That's an interesting story," Tom confessed. "It's really strange that Balaam would talk to his ass that way. But what's it got to do with me?"

"Well, I see it in a little different way," I said. "I think it's really strange that God spoke through the donkey to Balaam."

"Yes. But what's that got to do with us?" he insisted.

I paused for emphasis and looked squarely at Tom.

"If the Lord can speak through a dumb ass, He can speak through you!"

Tom's call to Mr. Carter carried an affirmative answer.

35

A going-away party had been called. It was to be a dessert potluck in the orchard. Amy was delighted. She could eat all the cakes and pies and cookies she wanted and wouldn't have to eat all her meat and vegetables first.

When the appointed evening came, everyone was there. They were very complimentary about our contribution to the valley. They wished us the best and asked us to please come back whenever we could. They also gave us a gift. It was a set of Corning Ware dishes. Darrell told us they had chosen plain white so that we would remember the Stehekin winters every time we used them. It was also to remind us to be pure as the "driven snow," especially in the city, where we might be tempted to be otherwise.

We were touched equally by the thoughts and by the gift. We would be keeping two households, one in Denver during the week and one in Nebraska on the weekend. We would need two sets of everything. Their gift was as practical as it was thoughtful. It spoke of the kind of people they were.

After the main festivities people broke into little groups here and there, some in Wendy and Phil's house, some under the trees, and others by the outdoor fireplace, roasting marshmallows. As twilight ended and the stars became brighter, Jody Stecher brought out his fiddle. At first he played lively fiddle songs. Some he sang as he played, his toe keeping time with the music. Amy and Sally got their quota of half-burnt marshmallows and ran off to play with the other kids. Tom and I sat down on a bench near the open fire. A half-moon lit the mountains in the background, silhouetting the apple trees. I saw the children playing chase through the orchard and heard their laughter and shouts of pleasure.

Jody began playing gentle, melodic tunes, songs that said to us, It's been a good life here!

My mind stretched back over the four years we had been here. What different people we had been then: anxious, fretful, striving, searching, adventuresome people. I thought of the events that had changed us so much, the big moments and the small ones. I saw how God had planned it all. No part of it was ever out of His control. Every moment of it was planned by Him for our growth and pleasure and fulfillment. Not once had He left us. He was with us even before we knew it.

I saw how Sally had gone from a child of five to a person who would soon be a young lady. She, too, had grown more independent in this valley. Her creative potential had been allowed to blossom. She had a beautiful and lively imagination, and the hours of playing in the woods and meadows had strengthened it. She had begun her walk with the Lord, too. Movingly and so sweetly she accepted Christ one afternoon while kneeling on the rug in front of the fire. What a precious person she was. What would city life mean to her? How would she learn to cope with it?

Amy. Dear Amy. She'd come here as a baby, only two years old. She didn't know any other way of life. What would the city seem like to her? Would her free spirit have to be bridled? How would she adjust to a school where neither her mother nor her father taught? She always had both of us with her.

And Tom. The tender music coming from Jody's fiddle wrapped around my heart as I thought of Tom. We had truly become one here in this place. How could I endure a life where we would be separated most of the day and even part of the night? I knew a minister's work was very demanding on a man's time. I was willing for him to give himself to God's work but ached to think that it would take him away from me for hours at a time. "Lord, help me with that, please."

Nebraska! The high, dry, rolling plains of Nebraska. What a contrast to our cozy mountain home. And how could I be a minister's wife? How could I play a role if I didn't know what it was? It was a pressing question. I had thought of it many times in the past weeks, and now, with the moon over our beloved valley that we would be leaving and the music from Jody's fiddle, I could no longer suppress the question.

"Tom," I said urgently. "I don't know how to be a minister's wife!"

He put his arm around me and pulled me close. By the firelight I could see his eyes, filled with love, looking deeply into mine. He smiled gently and said, "Sweetie Pie, don't you worry about how to be a minister's wife. Just go on being *my* wife. You certainly know how to do that."

His lips were as tender and loving as his eyes had been. How I loved being his wife!

36

The U-Haul truck was backed up to the side porch of the cabin. The truck had come in on the barge shortly after noon. We had until seven o'clock to get it packed and back to the barge. Tom and two other men worked steadily all afternoon.

At six o'clock Tom shouted, "Praise the Lord! She's all packed! And everything went in!"

His voice echoed through the empty house. The two helpers left as I closed the suitcase that would keep us until we arrived in Nebraska. My throat was choked with emotion. We were about to leave our valley!

I went out to sit on the grass in front of the empty cabin. I stared at "my" mountains, and tears flowed freely down my face. Tom dropped onto the grass beside me.

"Really tough to leave here, isn't it?" he said, looking around at the mountains and woods, the gardens and meadows.

"Um-hum," was all I could manage.

"It's been good here, real good! We've grown so much."

"You know," I sniffed, "I was reading in Deuteronomy this morning, Chapter eight. It says, 'And thou shalt remember all the way which the Lord thy God led thee these forty years in the wilderness, to humble thee, and to prove thee, and to know what was in thine heart, whether thou wouldest keep his commandments, or no.' That's exactly what has happened to us these four years. It's really hard to leave."

"Yes, but remember what God told Joshua when he was called to take over after Moses died. It was such a big job, to lead those straggly mobs into their new land. Joshua was afraid he couldn't do it, but God said to him, 'Have I not commanded thee? Be strong and of a good courage; be not afraid, neither be thou dismayed: for the Lord thy God is with thee whithersoever thou goest.'" (Josh. 1:9)

Later that evening, I stood at the edge of the lake and watched as the barge carried away the U-Haul with all our belongings. There it went. It was so final. We were really leaving. But even in the agony of the moment I realized how beautiful the scene was. The flat barge moved slowly down the lake. The bright orange stripe of the truck stood out in bright contrast with the grayness of the twilight. The steep, green-covered mountains were the backdrop; and the blue, sparkling water was the base. As the barge slipped slowly out of sight, I thought of another verse.

> O Lord God, thou hast begun to shew thy servant thy greatness, and thy mighty hand: for what God is there in heaven or in earth, that can do according to thy works, and according to thy might? (Deut. 3:24)

Amen, Lord, Amen.
And tomorrow I will be following a U-Haul truck again.